A Space for Race

OXFORD
UNIVERSITY PRESS

Oxford University Press is a department of the University of Oxford. It furthers
the University's objective of excellence in research, scholarship, and education
by publishing worldwide. Oxford is a registered trade mark of Oxford University
Press in the UK and certain other countries.

Published in the United States of America by Oxford University Press
198 Madison Avenue, New York, NY 10016, United States of America.

© Oxford University Press 2018

All rights reserved. No part of this publication may be reproduced, stored in
a retrieval system, or transmitted, in any form or by any means, without the
prior permission in writing of Oxford University Press, or as expressly permitted
by law, by license, or under terms agreed with the appropriate reproduction
rights organization. Inquiries concerning reproduction outside the scope of the
above should be sent to the Rights Department, Oxford University Press, at the
address above.

You must not circulate this work in any other form
and you must impose this same condition on any acquirer.

CIP data is on file at the Library of Congress
ISBN 978-0-19-085891-9

3 5 7 9 8 6 4 2

Printed by Webcom, Inc., Canada

A Space for Race

Decoding Racism, Multiculturalism, and Post-Colonialism in the Quest for Belonging in Canada and Beyond

KATHY HOGARTH

WENDY L. FLETCHER

OXFORD
UNIVERSITY PRESS

*This book is dedicated to every racialized
person who has struggled to find a place to belong.*

Contents

Preface   ix
Overview of the Book   xiii
About the Authors   xv
Introduction: On the Merits of Belonging and Unbelonging   xvii
    Kathy's Story   xvii
    Wendy's Story   xix
    Making the Personal Political   xx

1. Race, Racism, and Anti-Racism in Canada   1
    History of Racism in Western Culture and
        Canadian Immigration   2
    Canadian Context   6
    Canada's Black History   9
    New Immigrants and Refugees   11
    Muslim and Arab Canadians   13
    Change in the Legal Arena   16
    Anti-Racism   19

2. What's Post About Colonialism   23
    Canada and Colonization in Historical Perspective   24
    First Nations and Colonization in Canada   26
    Broad Limitations of the Indian Act   28
    Criminalization of Indigenous Culture   29
    Reserve Lands: An Exercise in Containment and Control   29
    Education as an Assimilationist Tool   30
    Colonial Reproductions: The Methods of Reinvention   37
    Conclusion   47

3. Belonging and Diaspora — 49

  Understanding Diaspora 52
  Space and Social Imaginary 52
  Immigration and Other Laws Defining Space by Race 55
  The Lens 56
  The Chinese Experience 57
  The Japanese Experience 60
  The Black Experience 63
  Challenges of Diaspora 64
  Shifting Notions of Diaspora 66
  Conclusion 69

4. Canadian Multiculturalism — 70

  Black Canadians 72
  Antisemitism and the Story of Jewish Canada 74
  Racialized Antisemitism 76
  Jewish Immigration 78
  The Tenor of Canadian Antisemitism 79
  A History of Arabs in Canada 81
  Islamophobia 82
  Difference, Belonging, and Multiculturalism 85

5. Moving Toward Belonging — 94

  First Nations Communities: An Exception
    That Proves the Rule 97
  Black Communities 101
  Jewish Communities 104
  Chinese Communities 106
  Japanese Communities 107
  Arab and Muslim Communities 108
  Expressions of Racism in a New Key 109

Notes — 113

References — 121

Index — 131

Preface

CANADA. A HUGE EXPANSE of land that is reflective of its motto *A Mari usque ad Mare*, which translates "From Sea to Sea." Embedded in this motto were both a proclamation of Canada's colonial mission and a signal of its multicultural ideal. During the time of Confederation, when this phrase came into being in Canada, "From Sea to Sea" only existed as a dream of geographical domination. At the time, the Dominion of Canada consisted only of Ontario, Quebec, Nova Scotia, and New Brunswick. "From Sea to Sea" did not geographically apply to Canada until 1871, when British Columbia joined the Confederation and the Dominion extended from the Atlantic Ocean to the Pacific Ocean.

The multicultural ideal embedded within the "From Sea to Sea" motto was realized in 1971 when Canada became the first country in the world to adopt multiculturalism as an official policy. Implicit within the domination of people is the construct of difference or the "Other." It is within this context of domination and multiculturalism that this text is written. These notions will be explored in greater detail throughout the text.

Canada continues with its immigration mission as a means of driving its growth and economic prosperity with plans of surpassing immigrant intake numbers of previous years. The continuing increases in the racialized immigrant population evoke the question of belonging: Who belongs or gets to belong and how is belonging negotiated? These questions, when contextualized within the White space, become particularly problematic for racialized immigrants. The project of colonization carried ideological norms on the back of economic expansion. The goal of economic expansion led to the expropriation of land for new raw materials and transportation access points. The expropriation of land and raw materials generated the need for "management" of peoples already in residence in the newly assumed land. Race, class, and gender enter the story, as three pillars of the people management strategy of colonial powers.

Our purpose in this text is to explore the theme of race and racialization in relation to societal harm and in some ways to puncture our consciousness about the "true north, strong and free." However, the exploration we undertake assumes our prior acknowledgment of this key point: Race, class, and gender were essentially intertwined as the primary categories of embedded social hierarchy. Colonizing powers, in our case the British Empire, had a worldview that set people in a hierarchical relation of value defined by the projection of their value system onto the broader world: White was the best color; male was the best gender; propertied and wealthy was the best status. It was assumed that the place of all would be determined by their relationship to these categories of value. White males with education and property assumed the right to make determinations, legal and otherwise, for all other "categories" of persons. And they did. This is reflected in the legalized system of racism, sexism, and exploitation of the poor that defined much of Canadian history. Here, we enter the story of this triumvirate of oppression primarily through the lens of race, understanding that it also implies the essentializing of the other categories as aspects of the social landscape.

> *Strategic essentialism*, a term coined by post-colonial feminist theorist Gayatri Spivak, refers to the unifying of otherwise distinct ethnicities on the basis of a shared identity in the public sphere as a means of strategically positioning marginalized populations.

As we enter, we attempt to strike the balance between homogeneity and *strategic essentialism* with a recognition that even "progressive" movements such as feminism have created a form of ethnocentric universalism which re-creates structures of dominance that suppress the individuality of the racialized Other. While we walk with a consciousness of the dangers cultural essentialism poses for the ethnic Other, we, at the same time, give attention to the value of strategic essentialism. It is these very waters we navigate as we speak of Arabs, Blacks, Jews, and Original peoples. We recognize that there are many complexities within these seemingly homogenized groups. That is, within the Black experience, for instance, there is a multiplicity of identities and so the experiences of a Black person originating from the Caribbean are much different from those of a Black person originating from the African continent and even different from those of a second- or third-generation Black Canadian. What we do want to reflect is that societal constructs of these groups are often homogenized and individuality is often invalidated.

The historical narratives contained herein are intended to aid our remembering of history. We have an ontology of forgetting, erasing, and rewriting history for the benefit of the dominant. In so doing, we invalidate the experiences of those who endured and continue to endure the atrocities of the colonial machinery, of oppression, and the long list of historical wrongs. It is our duty to not forget so that we can reimagine our future. To this end, we engage with history in a particular way that challenges the historical record that has informed our imaginings. We interrogate those historical accounts with the guiding questions of who was that history written about, by whom, and for whom? In many instances, we see that popular history has been written by a dominant society for the consumption of a dominant society and as such does not necessarily contain all the truth. For instance, we have many discovery narratives that form our collective history, and in those narratives "people" are often removed and replaced by "savages," as a means of asserting and justifying our supremacy as a White dominant society.

Not always evident throughout the book, religion remains in the background and helps frame our understanding in a very non-obvious way. As we contend with the issues of racism, post-colonialism, multiculturalism, and space making, one of the lightly colored threads woven throughout is that of religion. Religion expresses meaning, communicates value, and serves as a vehicle for the transmission of cultural norms. In this, it functions in Foucauldian terms as a hegemonic institution. As with education and the law, religious institutions serve both a function of formation and social control. Although the influence of religion in most Western cultures has significantly declined in the past decades, during the period of Canada's first centuries that was not the case.

> *Hegemony* refers to the notion of dominance and supremacy, especially in relation to social groups over others. In this regard, *"hegemonic"* is understood as the process by which the dominant culture maintains its dominant position.

Separation between church and state in British North America had been enshrined as a constitutional principle from 1852. However, the project of power holding as a social practice was shared in ways that it is difficult to conceive of today. Christian language as a norm was as assumed as racialized ideas and perhaps as the English language itself.

As a pillar of the power structures of the British Empire, and partner in the project of "civilization," Christianity articulated and purveyed not only theological norms but also social and cultural norms. The vision that Canada's original nation makers had was of a "Christian Canada." The involvement of the church in the project of nation building was unquestioned. As the project of assimilation arose in relation both to Indigenous peoples and to immigrants, including racialized minorities, the government looked to the church as its partner. Enthused to have such a broad and potentially dynamic social purpose, Christian churches jumped on board the assimilation train, anxious to be of use. The assumptions about race that both church and government brought to bear on its interactions with Original and immigrant Canadians were shared, embedded as they were in the general ideological framework of the age. This meant, then, that religion became, most often but not always, a willing participant in the project of racialized assimilation.

Overview of the Book

THROUGHOUT THE BOOK, we engage with various contested notions related to racialized other belonging in Canada. The book is composed of five chapters and uses race as the pivoting axis on which issues of post-colonialism, diaspora, multiculturalism, and belonging rests. Chapter 1 introduces the concept of race and glances through history in tracing its construction through to its current functioning. In Chapter 2, we adopt a Marxian view of colonialism and question the notion of the "colonial era" that undergirds an assumption that colonialism was a fixed period of time that is now past. In the process of questioning, we highlight some of the various forms in which colonialism is reinvented in the modern day and conclude that there is in fact nothing post about colonialism. Chapter 3 brings us to a discussion about "space making" and how various groups attempt to negotiate a sense of belonging as diasporic peoples and within diaspora. We explore further the shifting notions of diaspora and highlight some of the challenges linked to diasporic engagements. The concept of multiculturalism is the focus of Chapter 4. We use the discussion in this chapter to critically analyze the ideal as well as the current functioning of multiculturalism in Canada, again directing our analysis through various ethnic groups. In this chapter, we also problematize the normativeness of Whiteness situating the "White" norm as an inherent challenge to the ideal of multiculturalism. Chapter 5 draws the reader's attention to the many inroads that have been made despite the challenges associated with racism, colonialism, and multiculturalism in Canada.

About the Authors

KATHY HOGARTH, PHD, is Associate Professor in the School of Social Work at Renison University College, University of Waterloo. She holds a master's degree in Counselling Psychology, a master's degree in Community Psychology, and a PhD in Social Work. She currently teaches in the areas of diversity, integrating field practice and social work theory, program evaluation, and international social work. Her areas of research are focused on marginalization and oppression within systems with particular focus on immigrant and racialized populations. She serves on the board of directors for the Canadian Association of Social Work Educators (CASWE) in her capacity as Co-Chair of the International Affairs Committee for CASWE, and she co-chairs the Race and Ethnicity Caucus for CASWE.

WENDY L. FLETCHER is President and Vice-Chancellor of Renison University College, University of Waterloo. She is also Professor in Religious Studies at the University of Waterloo. Her research has explored the intersection of religion and culture with particular reference to social change and persistence. The impact of hegemonizing discourse on marginalized populations in Western culture, notably women and racialized minorities generally, and the impact of colonization on Indigenous communities have been the most recent foci of her work. She descends from the peoples of Newfoundland, Ireland, Scotland, and the Ojibway and Mohawk Nations. She was adopted into the Lakota nation with the name Wanbli Wiyaka Win (Eagle Feather Woman). She was also adopted into the Raven crest of the Haida House of Kyaanuusalii (Codfish People from the Star House). She carries the name Yaahl Xuhlyang (Shining Raven).

Introduction

ON THE MERITS OF BELONGING AND UNBELONGING

Kathy's Story

2008 was a rough year. My husband had been unemployed for most of the time. When he did manage to get employment, he was grossly underemployed or working at the mercy of employers on contracts, some of which promised to last for 6–9 months but ended abruptly, one lasting only 4 days. In two instances, after a successful phone interview and an invitation to visit the business to complete the paperwork, the positions suddenly became unavailable once he presented in person. We believed racism was at play in most of these instances but could not call it such because we had no grounds on which to make such claims. Often, many of his job interviews were done by telephone without the face-to-face interaction. Voice has no color, yet the presence of a Black man somehow seemed to erase his suitability for a position for which he was once otherwise highly qualified. Nonetheless, by the end of the year we found ourselves relying on the food bank. We were advised to register for a Christmas hamper so that our kids would get some toys for Christmas and we would have some food.

It was a snowy morning in early December when I approached the Salvation Army to register for the Christmas hamper. There was a line of people waiting outside closed doors. With the exception of one, all were women. I joined the line. A few minutes later, I tapped the shoulder of the lady in front of me and asked, "What is this line for?" She bent her head down, turned to the side, and whispered "Bread." Since I was not there for bread, I skipped the line and went inside the building. There was a woman standing guard at the door. Part of her responsibility was to let in those in the line when space became available inside. It was not a very large room. There were about seven people in the room not including the three workers. About three people were let in at a time. As one entered the room, straight ahead there was a White woman behind a reception-like area. She was responsible for doling out nonperishable food items and fruits. Once that was done, a few steps to the left was a shelf with bread where people could go and select the bread they wanted. And a few steps to the left of that was a little desk where I sat as I filled out the registration for the Christmas hamper.

The shout of "One bread please, you are only allowed one bread" echoed through the room as the White woman acting as security at the door attempted to correct a wrong that was taking place at the bread shelf. All eyes turned their gaze to the woman in the hijab and her son who had taken up a mini baguette, a sliced loaf and a naan. With a look of great embarrassment, the woman and her son quietly returned the breads and made a hasty decision about which one they should take and then they left.

The pleasant-looking White woman who had given me the forms to fill out returned and sat behind the desk. She began to ask questions about my needs. "Are you on welfare?" she asked. "No, I'm a student." "Do you receive OSAP?" "Yes." "Are you single?" "No." "Is your husband employed?" "No." "Is he receiving E.I.?" "No." "What is your source of income?" "OSAP." "You need to kick him in the butt to get out there and find a job." The look of disdain on my face probably spoke volumes to her and she replied, "Oh I'm only joking." "He is unemployed not for lack of trying" I said and then thought to myself that I really did not need to justify myself to this woman. In an attempt to redeem herself, she asked "What kind of job is he looking for?" "Accounting," I replied. "Oh has he tried RIM? My husband just found a job there, maybe you should get him to try RIM." Having already resigned myself from this conversation, I said "Sure." She then proceeded to tell me when the hamper would be available and that I needed to return with identification for my 8-month-old.[1]

The previously outlined experience left me with a series of questions. What is it that made the lady in the line feel the need to whisper even though everybody else in the line was there for the same purpose? Why is it that in a city in which the immigrant and refugee population stands at 22%, every person accessing the services of the food bank at that moment was a racialized minority? What justified the humiliating actions of the service provider that further eroded the dignity of the woman in the hijab, and what is the impact of this experience on her son? Why was it that the White worker who was dealing with my case assumed to know the reasons for my predicament and dared to even voice it? Put together, these are dislocating experiences that are gendered, classed, and raced. They highlight grave inequities in the system, and such iniquitous and dislocating experiences serve to undermine any sense of true integration into the Canadian society. Equally important and central to this work, this experience highlighted how "Whiteness" is normed in Canadian society and how these everyday occurrences further entrench stereotypical presumptions about people of color being, among others, lazy, and dependent on the goodwill of the state for survival.

Wendy's Story

I was born in 1963 to a 14-year-old mother. In 1964, I was adopted by the Fletchers, an Anglo-speaking family with English roots, and grew up during my earliest year in Brantford, Ontario, near the 6 Nations reserve. Given the laws in Ontario regarding adoption disclosure at the time, it was many decades before I learned anything of substance about my biological heritage. Diverse threads made me. Two of those threads include Ojibway and Mohawk ancestry.

About 20 years ago, I was scooped up in an unplanned way into the world of First Nations peoples. I spent 15 years on the West Coast working in a graduate school connected to the University of British Columbia which had an Indigenous Studies program that had been developing for more than two decades when I joined. For the 15 years I spent in Vancouver, my work with Indigenous students, scholars, and communities became the central preoccupation of my working life.

Immersion in the world of my new relatives led to my adoption first by the Sicangu Lakota First Nation. I was given the name Wanbliwiakawin (Eagle Feather Woman). Somewhat later I was adopted also by the Kyaanuusli Raven House of the Haida First Nation and given the name Yuul Kyulaanx (Shining Raven). Adopted first into a new community of belonging as a child, I found myself in my 40s again welcomed into new families, new communities of belonging. To be ceremonially adopted is a critical ritual for First Nations communities. An entire Indigenous community discerns one's eligibility. The ceremony is one of the most sacred and guarded transformations in any First Nation. When one is adopted, it cannot be broken, unlike any other human relationship. With adoption, both the privileges and the obligations of belonging are confirmed.

In the course of my work at the university, I was cross appointed to the School of Social Work, in light of my Indigenous background and experience. Work was needed in developing that dimension of our program. I accepted an invitation from the department to develop a course in Indigenous Health. Unbeknownst to me, questions were raised about the appropriateness of my leadership for the course. Surely, we needed Indigenous leadership. When I heard about the conversation, I was shocked. I am Indigenous. Did not everyone understand that? What right did anyone have to question my legitimacy to work in the First Nations world?

The strength of my emotional reaction took me by surprise. During my time at Waterloo, there had been virtually no point of contact with First Nations communities or work. What had been at the center of my world for so long now barely touched its edge. Even so, it had never occurred to me that people did not understand me as I understood myself.

At a subsequent meeting with the department, we discussed the question of who I understood myself to be. I was shocked to realize people had very little, if any, sense of my background. But then I saw: I myself have been silent. Living in my new world, diverse in some ways and not in others, I presented as who I had been raised to be: Wendy Fletcher, educated, capable, inheritor of the benefits of White privilege. I had been silent about the other Wendy. Why, I asked myself, had I been silent? I realize that there are two reasons for my silence. The first is my worry that in presuming to name my First Nations identity, I would benefit from the current political climate that values Indigenous voice in the academy while never having suffered, as my relatives had, from the limitations of racial marginalization. The second reason for my silence was an apprehension that to speak of my Indigenous identity would be to displace my privilege and power, in ways that would be difficult to measure given the political climate of the day, but nonetheless real.

It was only when someone outside of the Indigenous community dared to question my right to teach in the area of Indigenous life that who I was stood up in me. For me not to own all the parts of who I am and the story that has made me is to dishonor not only where I come from but also the people who have loved, named, and owned me—the Fletchers, the Lakota Nation, the Haida Nation—and the parts of me (largely not yet owned) in the story of my heritage. Yet, as I risk laying claim to my Indigenous heritage, I also must come to terms with the power I gained as I rode on the coattails of White privilege. Power and position that often give rise to the questions my colleagues entertained about my appropriateness to develop and teach a course in the area of Indigeneity.

Making the Personal Political

I daresay that in today's Canada I am not atypical. The complicated story of how we become who we are is not straightforward for most of us. For me, then, this is where the conversation must begin: unpacking the complicated threads of diversity, which make this nation. Multiculturalism, racialized unbelonging, racially defined belonging is a complicated and painful story, the interpretation of which gives us some place to begin in imagining the society we intend to leave as a legacy for the generations that will follow us.

What is the purpose of such personal stories to introduce the contents of this book? Stories hold important questions. They ground. They provide necessary links between the personal and the political, between the micro and the macro, and between the past and the present. One of the challenges of writing in this particular area of scholarship often resides in the spaces between the personal and the political. How does the personal connect with the political; the micro with the macro? We approached this work with the underlying principle that the personal is the political; that the micro issues and experiences impact in significant ways at the macro level and vice versa; that the individual experiences are tightly woven in the collective. Furthermore, we believe that as we track and tackle issues of race, we must insist on contextualizing it, in connecting the past to the present and the individual to the system. To this end, we provide the reader with several case studies that traverse both the personal and the systems levels and draw our gaze toward the intersections between these levels.

On Fighting the Beast

Racism stands as a formidable beast before us. It is not a new image on our horizon
It's been crouching, growling; sometimes asleep, just beneath the surface of our everyday
Soothed by the game of improvement, covered by blankets of sensitivity, all the while breathing in new life
Engorged by our complacency, tickled by our naivety, inseminating us and breeding new life
There is no neutral ground.
There is no safe space—we are either feeding it or fighting it
How do we attack this formidable beast before us?
It first starts with recognizing the beast before us
Dropping our pretenses that it does not exist or maybe it's not as bad
Those who suffer in the grips of its fangs know the terrible bite
Those who are submerged just below the surface gaze at its ugliness in perpetual motion
How do we attack this formidable beast before us?
We peel back our sensitivity blankets, and dismantle our safe spaces recognizing that these blankets and spaces are only for the benefit of those not caught in the grip of the beast
And we bravely march towards the horizon.

—Kathy Hogarth

A Space for Race

I

Race, Racism, and Anti-Racism in Canada

THE FACT THAT racism exists is undeniable if one is open to looking with even less than a critical eye and question, ever so slightly, some of the structures and practices that exist in our society. Disparities in the health, education, and judicial systems all indicate that we do not exist in a racially egalitarian society. Far from a new phenomenon, empirical data highlight the deep-seated racism that has informed Canadian society throughout history and continues to do so today. Affirming the existence of race and racism is a critical undertaking particularly given our current climate of political correctness. Without such an affirmation of its existence, race is likely to become diluted and lose its saliency amid more palatable terms such as culture, ethnicity, and diversity.

The discussion in this chapter begins with a historical examination of racism, its origins, and its beginning place in the Canadian narrative and an attempt to contextualize it in contemporary society. The central construction under examination in this chapter is racism and as such requires definition. Race is understood to be a social construct, a means of classifying or differentiating one group of people from another. Racism, flowing from the construct of race, is the use of racial categories to create, explain, and perpetuate inequalities. The centrality of racism lies in the perpetuation of inequalities or the differentiation of treatment based on perceived racial differences. Its defining characteristics rest in both attitude and actions that oppress and marginalize individuals and groups of people as a result of phenotypical differences.

To address issues of race, necessarily one must engage notions of the racialized and racialization—terms that have become commonplace in race discourse but that often lack a sharp conceptualization. These notions are not the same, as one speaks to subjectivities and the other to a process of signification. It is also important to note that the process of racialization can be applied to all, including the privileged and dominant (i.e., dominant groups racialized for privilege and power; and the question of who has the power to racialize the other as different is also key here). The term *racialized* is used to emphasize the fact that racial categories are socially constructed: It refers to the discursive production of racial identities. The term is used to enact categorization or differentiation on the basis of race. It expands on Simone de Beauvoir's existentialist notion[1] that existence precedes essence and that one is not born racialized, but over the course of time one becomes racialized. Although we are born with the physical characteristics of color, race in itself is defined and "becomes," as in an interactional process. In that process of becoming, we train people up to be "Othered" and oppositional. The term racialized is double-edged in that on one end it relates to the politics of identity as in the individual "becoming Black"—the consciousness and embracing of my own Blackness—whereas on the other end it refers to the majority society imposing a racial interpretation on another, whether or not that racialized identity is embraced by the "Other."

History of Racism in Western Culture and Canadian Immigration

The idea of race and the practice of racism are so pervasive in Western culture that we assume they have been with us always. This is a misplaced assumption. Although xenophobia and oppression of particular groups have always been present within human cultures, the idea of race and the use of that idea as a tool of oppression, as the reason for "othering," are an invention of the modern era.

The idea of race has its roots in the Enlightenment of the 18th century and the period of religious revival that accompanied it. The juxtaposition of these two phenomena seems contraindicated. The Enlightenment was a reaction against the perceived irrationality of religious experience and the superstition that was associated with religious belief. With the rise of early science in the period that both preceded and overlapped with the Enlightenment, Western intellectual life became preoccupied with the idea of a rational universe. The Pietism of 18th-century Europe, on the other hand, emphasized emotion as a primary category for basing epistemological claims. The rationalism of the Enlightenment and the emotionalism of Pietism as a religious revival movement that fueled the social imagination toward the possibility of a new world were a potent combination. This partnership created the context first for the development of the idea of race and then the subsequent idealization of the idea of race as a romantic category that fueled utopian notions of an ideal society. The myth implicit in that ideal when placed in the hands of historical actors, particularly through the colonial enterprise, concretized in social forms. Thinkers imagined a world in which Caucasians were the ideal type and then put the myth of superiority into historical practice through legal, political, and economic actions. We know this as racism.

Enlightenment thinkers were driven to categorization. Plants, animals, phenomena of all kinds fell within the scope of this rationalizing project. Defining elements, events, people, and things was the intellectual vehicle for understanding their value and meaning. Knowing what something's place was in the order of things created the ideal of an ordered society—an order that intentionally aimed at supplanting the more chaotic social vision of a world grounded in superstition with forces beyond human control.

It is not possible to posit a fixed point in time for the beginning of the developing worldview of racism. However, we do know that the word "race" has existed in the English language since the Renaissance. In its earliest usage, it did not refer uniquely to types of people but, rather, to categories of things more broadly, including nations, animals, and family traits. There was no linkage of the term yet to a connotation of better and worse, higher and lower, inferior and superior. The earliest version of an idea of race as a category of people linked to blood has to be posited in relation to Jewish ancestry. As early as the 16th century in Spain, the idea of "purity of blood" was used to justify discrimination against Jewish people (Mosse, 1978, p. xv). However, the express linkage of the idea of race that fused the outward appearance of human beings with their place in nature and the functioning of their soul, as well as their value and meaning, was a later development.

We see the term *race* used first in the English language in 1508 in a poem by William Dunbar, in which he uses the term to talk about a "race of things." The beginning place of this word in the world of poetry is important because it connotes what would become its first usage, which was as a romantic ideal. Although the word migrates into the "rational" field of Enlightenment discourse, its place in poetic and literary usage throughout the 17th and 18th centuries means that it carries with it a form of romantic idealism. When Western thinkers first used the idea of race to denote categories of human beings in the late 18th century, it was largely with an ideal romanticism in mind. For example, newly "discovered" Indigenous persons of the Americas were identified as different in the racial hierarchy but "noble" rather than degenerate as they would become in a later century. We see the poignancy of this romanticism clearly delineated in Rousseau's (1754) *A Discourse on Inequality*, which postulated a purity of spirit in newly discovered persons, who were notably different from Europeans. His writing expressed a nostalgia for a premodern idyllic state, lost in the push toward change in the early modern era. Publishing his thinking only a decade after Rousseau, Immanuel Kant (1764/1961), in his famous tract *Observations on the Feeling of the Beautiful and the Sublime*, was most likely the first to explicitly use the term race in the sense of biologically or physically distinctive categories of human beings.

At the same time as literary figures wrote and philosophers reflected, the emerging world of medical science and anthropology opened the door on the invention of racial classification (Stuurman, 2000). Francois Bernier wrote an anthropological essay in the late 18th century that experimented with the idea of discussing human beings according to varieties. Most important about Bernier's work is that it served as a linchpin for later thinking developed in the thought of persons such as French anatomist Georges Cuvier (1769–1832), who took the experimental idea of racial classification to new climes through his postulation of three major races of human beings: white, yellow, and black. Writing in 1805, Cuvier suggested that the simplest means of defining human variation should be based on skin color. It was his belief that all human beings were descended from the Caucasian or white race and that the skin color of the other two groups shifted after a major catastrophe several thousand years prior had led to their geographic separation from the Caucasians. Given his view that "White" was the original race, he began the process of stratifying the value of human races by color. Cuvier (1789) wrote, "The white race with oval face, straight hair and nose, to which the civilized people of Europe belong and which appear to us the most beautiful of all, is also superior to others, by its genius, courage and activity" (p. 71).

In the decades that followed the development of theories of race through thinkers such as Bernier, Western powers co-opted these theories and used them to serve the displacement of persons as necessary in the broader project of colonial expansion. All the major powers of Europe embarked on the project of colonial expansion to various corners of the globe. Everywhere persons were encountered who were different than the defined normativity of the "White" person, theories of racial classification that lent superiority to the Whites were applied. Whether it was Africa, Asia, or the Americas, the broader concept of race was linked both to class and to economic power, and persons who fell outside of the Euro-descent classification were understood as either dispensable or to be used in the service of the broader economic interests of the colonizing power. Gone was the idea of idealized and noble savage of 18th-century literature. It was replaced with the categorization of Indigenous persons as ignorant savages who could be used and displaced at will by the fierce engine of 19th-century colonial activity. Persons in Africa and Asia were also seen as fodder for enslavement of various kinds based solely on the assumption of their inferiority by racial classification. Understanding that the continent of Europe had, with the Enlightenment, discovered the idea of the rights of the human being broadly speaking, had persons resident in the continents encountered through colonial expansion been seen as human beings, as equal to the colonizer, they could not have easily been supplanted, dominated, oppressed, and replaced, and the political economic project of colonization could not have been achieved.

The notion of race assumes that humanity is divided into unchanging natural types recognizable by physical features and transmitted through "blood" or genetic inheritance. Racism, as distinct from race, is the use of the idea of race for the subjugation of some groups by others based on the imagined notion of the classification of human beings by physical type, beginning with skin color and other physical features but extending to the interior life, making pronouncement about meaning and value: the intellectual, emotional, and spiritual value of human beings in gradation. The term ultimately implies that the mental and moral activity of human beings as well as individual personality, ideas, and capacities are related to racial origin and that race provides a satisfactory account of behavior. With this reconstruction of the chain of being according to racial categories and its application through global expansion (i.e., domination), early racial theorists attempted to create a utopia—an ideal society in which all would be conformed in some fashion to the ideal of Euro descent normativity. For this project, the enthusiasm of the religionists of the age was needed, and so churches and government partnered in the project of the suppression of and then the hoped for assimilation and renovation of the inferior other, as defined by their racialized value system, wherever colonizers went.

As such, we see that the division of human society by racial classification was inextricable from the need of colonizing powers to establish dominance over subject peoples. Although race was not an invention of imperialism, it quickly became one of its most supportive ideas. The idea of "White" superiority generated the emergence of race as a concept that was easily adapted to both impulses of colonization: dominance for economic reasons, on the one hand, and the idea of enlightenment, on the other hand—the raising up of subject peoples to the civilized state of the colonizer, in the name of making a whole world in the image of the colonizer.

Canadian Context

In the Canadian context, we can observe the practice of racism applied in two particular ways: One with reference to Original peoples who were displaced by colonization and the second with immigrant peoples who fall outside of the "Euro-decent Caucasian" classification, who are marginalized upon arrival in their new country. Subsequent chapters detail the particulars of that story. However, to lay the table for that narrative here, we consider the timelines around movement of peoples: arrivals that both displaced Indigenous persons and put the first markers on the map for Euro domination that would last as a normative hermeneutical lens until the last part of the 20th century.

The story of the colonization of the country that would become Canada is distinct from but related to the colonization of the United States of America in two key respects: Canada was first colonized by the French, and Canada remained loyal to Britain through and after the American Revolution. Both of these realities affected the story of how things went with Original peoples and immigrants over time.

A historical chronology of the colonizing process is provided to enrich our understanding of our present-day context. In 1759, the British defeated the French at the Battle of the Plains of Abraham. The famed Seven Years' War, which preoccupied European powers at home and throughout the world, ended in 1763. From 1763, the land now known as Canada was named British North America (BNA) and was added to the list of British foreign colonial interests. In 1776, the Thirteen Colonies to the south officially declared their nationhood after the American War of Independence, separating from Britain. This is of importance to our story in that the first significant migration of persons who would supplant Indigenous peoples began after that date. Persons of British heritage who had been loyal to the British Crown through the wars of independence began migrating north into what became Upper Canada (predominantly English-speaking territory as distinct from Lower Canada, which retained the legacy of its prior French colonization). The first significant influx of immigrants to BNA were English-speaking British loyalists. Interestingly, some of these loyalists were in fact Indigenous groups who had fought with the British in the War of Independence. This meant that some of the land that was re-designated for settlers was for Indigenous settlers, whose peoples had not been in that territory before. Notably, the land that was given, known as the Six Nations Reserve, was good farmland and provided an opportunity for the Six Nations to build a strong economic future for their people, unlike many of the displaced Indigenous nations that were moved further north over time.

Throughout the 19th century, British immigration into BNA continued at significant levels. Changes in the sociopolitical and economic climates both at home and abroad led to waves of immigration to the BNA. After 1815, the flow of immigrants from Britain was continuous. In the generation after 1815 (after the defeat of the Americans in 1812 who had tried to take over BNA), a large flood of immigration meant that immigration to the eastern colonies of Upper Canada was virtually complete. British plans for economic expansion in BNA, however, required an increase in population also of the western part of the land mass. Between 1841 and 1851, the population in the west nearly doubled from 455,688 to 952,004. This was largely due to British immigration. During this time, the Irish potato famines between 1845 and 1849 also fueled immigration to BNA, and in 1847 alone, more than 100,000 immigrants left Ireland for a new home across the Atlantic Ocean. These large-scale transatlantic movements laid the foundation for an English-speaking hegemony in what would become the new Canada in 1867. The lens of normativity for the new nation was framed in this period and by this immigration.

> Paul Cardan (Cornelius Castoriadis) first began writing about social imaginaries in the 1950s. For Castoriadis, being is self- and collective-creation. This creation occurs through both representing (language) and doing (praxis). In these processes, imagination is salient because representation and action can never be reduced to reason but always include a symbolic excess.

With Confederation in 1867, much changed. We discuss the form of this change in Chapter 2, as we explore the impact of colonization on Canada's Indigenous peoples. However, for our purposes here, it is important to note that a large flood of British immigration continued, parallel to the displacement of Indigenous communities, right up to the beginning of World War I. Others did come to Canada from marginalized groups (as per the racialization of the *social imaginary*)—for example, the Chinese. However, that immigration was circumscribed in very particular ways, which we explore in Chapter 3. Laying the power base for the new Canada were the British (Bodvarsson & Van den Berg, 2009, p. 413). After a depression that affected the world in the 1890s, expansion of the British Empire continued and with it came its people. Between 1890 and 1910, Canada's gross domestic product increased by 122% largely due to British immigration. A cycle of wet years beginning in 1899 made for an agricultural boom in the west that served as a catalyst for even further economic growth. Of course, this agricultural boom was on land taken through the displacement of non-agricultural First Nations communities. With the turn of the 20th century, immigration from predominantly English-speaking areas (with some Caucasian Eastern European immigration) spiked sharply, with more than 1 million people flooding into the Prairie Provinces alone between 1901 and 1911.

By the period of extensive 19th-century immigration, there was a clearly racialized social imaginary in place in Canada. This is notable both in immigration policies (who was allowed to come to Canada) and in how original persons were treated by those who came—as inferior and dispensable. This trend continued as the new century unfolded and as Canada put into place laws with regard to immigration that would limit undesirables by categories of race from entering the country.

In 1910, the parliament of Canada passed a new immigration act that significantly increased the discretionary power of the government in formulating selective entry decisions. With this act, the government was given legal authority to prohibit immigrants "belonging to any race deemed unsuited to the climate or requirements of Canada" (Bodvarsson & Van den Berg, 2009, p. 413). The climate requirement was designed to exclude persons from countries that were not northern, ostensibly arguing that they would find the climate too cold. However, the actual prohibition was for race, not geographic suitability. In 1923, Canada used its authority under this parliamentary act to limit the entry of immigrants to those who were British subjects or Americans, or who were from "preferred countries expressly named as Norway, Sweden, Denmark, Finland, Luxembourg, Germany, Switzerland, Holland, Belgium and France. From Eastern European countries such as Hungary, Poland, Romania and Yugoslavia among others, only agricultural labourers, women domestic servants and sponsored family members could enter" (Bodvarsson & Van den Berg, 2009, p. 413).

After World War II, immigration policy began to shift. Under the leadership of Prime Minister Mackenzie King, the "objectionable discrimination" of prior versions of immigration policy was flagged and some movement toward change began. However, it would be an overestimation of his contribution to suggest that he advocated the abolition of discrimination. Maintaining a "balanced" racial composition in Canadian society was still King's goal. He wrote (as quoted in Bodvarsson & Van den Berg, 2009, p. 414, referencing the work by Geoff Dench, "The New East End: Kinship, Race and Conflict" Profile Books, 2006), "The people of Canada do not wish as a result of mass immigration to make a fundamental alteration in the character of our population. Large-scale immigration from the orient would change the fundamental composition of the Canadian population."

The events of World War II affected the Canadian view of key issues such as basic human rights. As such, changes in the racialized social imaginary began to emerge. For the first time, Canada began the process of introducing a refugee policy, which prior to the war it had not had. At the time, all refugees were compelled to apply for entry under the immigration policy as it existed. As well, the number of immigrants allowed into the country opened up, in part because of a new and emerging view of human rights and in part because of the rapid economic expansion that was unfolding in Canada after the war. New immigrants were viewed as less of a threat to the economy and more as potential contributors. However, as we note in our discussion of First Nations challenges, the fact that Canada signed the United Nations' *Universal Declaration of Human Rights* in 1948 did not affect how it treated Indigenous and other minorities for decades after the signing.

Canada's Black History

From the historical sketch of racism in Canada, it can be seen that Canada has had a long history of institutionalized racism. This racism is practiced, with varying levels of intensity, against every ethnic group different from the White majority. In the ensuing chapters, we detail aspects of this disturbing story with reference to Indigenous persons and Jewish and Asian Canadians. Here, we frame the conversation as a beginning place with reference to Black Canadians. As chronicled by the Ontario Human Rights Commission (2005), Black slavery was actively practiced between 1628 and the early 1800s, and legislated segregation formed part of Canadian society until 1964. Blacks in Canada have had a particularly turbulent existence. The subjugation of Black bodies through slavery was one of the most blatant forms of racism to ever take place in the history of our existence, and Canada was no less complicit in slavery than France, Britain, or the United States. The first recorded history of Black slaves in Canada was in 1632, although evidence suggests the presence of Black slaves as early as 1607. Slavery was officially legalized in Canada between 1689 and 1709[2] and continued until official abolishment on August 1, 1833 (Trudel, 1994).

The 1834 official commencement of the abolition of slavery had very little impact on ending racism in Canada. The abolishment of slavery was followed by more than 100 years of legalized segregation with the "Common School Act" of 1850 enshrining segregated schools and classrooms, the segregated combat units in armed forces, and segregated public spaces that disallowed for comingling of Blacks and Whites. These policies were eventually recognized as explicitly racist, and de-legislation of racism followed with the last segregated school closing in 1983.[3]

Just as abolition of slavery had little impact on racism, so too did "desegregation" or the "deracializing" of Canadian policies on halting racism in Canada. In fact, efforts at deracializing served to embed racism as a hidden activity in the fabric of the society and, in some senses, as such it has become a normal part of everyday life. Although Canada has ideologically deracialized the racial discourse by not explicitly using racist or racial categories, nevertheless this discourse may, and often does, have racist effect. The literature during the past several decades has highlighted this very notion. For example, Walker (1985) noted that although "legal reforms have restrained openly hostile behaviour, they have not affected the essential factors leading to discrimination.... The basic issue in Canada has been racial stereotyping" (p. 24).

Canada's historical engagement with anti-Black racism has, in significant ways, informed Canadian national consciousness, and much of the discourse on the history of Blacks in Canada is closely linked to tales of Canada being a refuge to Blacks pre-Civil War. Although there is some truth to Canada's refugee granting status, there is also an inconvenient truth often hidden within that image. The truth of the Underground Railroad fostered a myth that the North Star led not only out of slavery but also into freedom, equality, and full participation in Canadian life. This myth became a liability for Canada, and it continues to prevent any sincere examination of the situation faced by Blacks and other racialized minorities. Our collective memories are filtered through a process of willful erasure and rewriting, so much so that we honestly cannot remember history in the same way. As a result, we come to the idealized and romanticized notions of nationhood and identity, which significantly impact our civic discourse.

The experiences, histories, and cultural engagements of Black Canadians challenge the myth that Canada is a racially benevolent and tolerant state when taking into consideration issues of institutional racism against Blacks in every facet of society and the everyday effects of such experiences. Traditional institutions of racialized research largely ignore the disparate social and political exposures confronting people of color, such as residential and occupational segregation, racial profiling, tokenism, discrimination, racism, and the consequential physiological and psychological effects flowing from the macro and micro effects of such interactions and intersectionalities. Many race scholars unsettle the origins of Canada's racist history and collusion of various social institutions in the perpetuation of the trope of "Black dangerousness." Media representations of Black bodies undeniably help maintain and perpetuate a particular ideology of Blacks that is closely linked to crime and aggression. These portrayals frame a national consciousness that is then replicated in everyday life. Police brutality and criminalization of Blackness are vivid examples of the impact such constructions of Blackness continue to have in Canadian society. Blacks account for 2.5% of Canada's population, but they account for 9% of the federal prison population. Is this overrepresentation of Blacks in prison really a matter of Blacks having greater criminogenic tendencies and acting them out? Similarly, there is a significant underrepresentation of Blacks in nonprecarious employment in Canada. Is it really that Blacks are just lazy and do not possess the inner drive to strive for better and greater employment opportunities? Or, what of the significant disparities in health? Is it that Blacks are truly biologically inferior to other ethnic groups and so are more susceptible to disease and ill health? Rhetorical as these questions may seem, they bear significance in that they cause us to pause and question some of the latent assumptions embedded in societal structures.

Blacks are by no means the only ethnic group that has endured and continues to live the experiences of racism in Canada, and in Chapter 3 we discuss the experiences and impact of racism on other ethnic groups. However, our current political climate warrants special attention on two particular groupings: immigrants and refugees and Muslim and Arabs. Increasingly, the presence of these two groups seem to be fueling a discourse in which the rhetoric about terrorism and cultural accommodation play a prominent role. This rhetoric forms part of the racist landscape.

New Immigrants and Refugees

Although historically Canada has actively engaged in anti-immigration racism, racism continues to be directed, in changing ways, at new immigrant groups, including those with ethnic backgrounds that no longer face overt discrimination in Canada today. Rooted in a deep existential fear of the "Other," anti-immigrant racism informs our understanding of Canadian national identity, and the Canadian discourse on immigrants is used to affirm White identity. Examining Canada's immigration discourse, there is a clear racial subtext through codified concepts and implied logic used to convey racial messages that appear not to be "race" based. Couched in the language of "safety" and the disintegration of national identity, racism becomes further embedded in policies and approaches toward immigrants and refugees. To some extent, the Canadian landscape still echoes the sentiments of the Director of Immigration in 1955, who stated (as quoted in Calliste, 1991),

> It is from experience, generally speaking, that coloured people in the present state of the white man's thinking are not a tangible asset, and as a result are more or less ostracised. . . . To enter into an agreement which would have the effect of increasing coloured immigration to this country would be an act of misguided generosity since it would not have the effect of bringing about a worthwhile solution to the problem of coloured people and would quite likely intensify our own social and economic problems. (p. 136)

Trends in polls from 2005 to the present show a steady increase in anti-immigration racism, with opposition to racialized immigrant migration being at an all-time high.[4] This trend was borne out in federal government support to deny health and social assistance to refugee claimants, which was legitimized in policy, thus creating a dichotomy of the "bogus" or "fraudulent" refugee and the "good" refugee.

In addition to the anti-immigrant racist rhetoric impacting policies, there is a significant impact of racism on the everyday lives of immigrants and refugees in Canada. The deeply entrenched nature of systemic racism in Canadian society acts as an effective barrier to integration for many racialized people. Differences in skin color and ethnicity are viewed as one of the factors used to effectively exclude racialized immigrants from the workforce and maintain their marginalized status in society. Race serves as a crucial factor influencing successful integration of racialized immigrants, and the significant negative effect that the experience of prejudice and discrimination has on a person's well-being clearly defines racism as a serious problem and risk factor facing immigrants and their mental health.

The recent refugee crisis and continuing immigration trends give a fair indication that Canada's racialized immigrant and refugee population will continue to increase despite the rhetoric of safety and loss of national identity. Unfortunately, the ongoing refugee crisis also heightens and perpetuates xenophobia and the fear of a refugee (read Muslim) takeover. The increases in immigrant and refugee intakes, however, evoke the question of belonging: Who belongs or gets to belong and how is belonging negotiated amid such strong anti-immigrant racism? These questions, when contextualized within the framework of minority/majority relations, become particularly problematic for racialized immigrants.

Muslim and Arab Canadians

The Muslim population in Canada has increased exponentially during the past two decades. Much of the increase in this population is a result of immigration.[5] Muslim reality in Canada is one lived amid an ever increasing level of fear, terror and accusations of terrorism, reprisals, and blame. Anti-Arab and anti-Muslim discourse, although indeed exacerbated in a post-September 11, 2001 (9/11) environment, is not a new phenomenon in Canada and appears to have started in earnest during the first Gulf War. Here, it is important to note that similar to antisemitism, anti-Muslim or Islamophobic attacks are most often racialized. Canadians of Arab or Muslim background became the targets of hostility, harassment, and racism when the Canadian government went to war against Iraq in 1991. In the post-9/11 Canada, Muslims and Arabs began to endure various forms of discrimination.[6]

The increasing discrimination and racism toward Muslims in Canada have not gone unnoticed. Racist constructions of Muslims and Arabs in Canadian media after 9/11 contribute to the racist environment, and there have been increases in racial profiling in the context of law enforcement and racist anti-terrorism initiatives after 9/11. Hanniman (2008) puts forth a unique explanation for the infiltration and surveillance suffered by Canada's Muslim citizens. According to Hanniman, the isolation and marginalization of Canada's Muslim citizens after the anti-Muslim reaction to 9/11 led to a security vulnerability in Muslim communities that needed to be addressed by the Royal Canadian Mounted Police.

The global media has consistently portrayed Islam as a religion prone to violence and Muslims as haters of the West. There is little attempt to separate the practice of religion from the practice of violence. Important in such portrayals is that Muslim values are antithetical to Canadian values. Such portrayals serve multiple purposes, not the least of which is to heighten Islamophobia reactions and shape public opinion and discourse. The danger discourse of the Arab Other exists even amid government posturing with Syrian refugees and the Canadian government's commitment to resettle these refugees. In a recent unveiling, Prime Minister Justin Trudeau conceded that the original plans to resettle 25,000 Syrian refugees by the end of 2016 must necessarily be altered given the

Canadian population's increased perception of risk. According to Trudeau (as quoted in Clark, 2015), "Canadians who have been extremely supportive and open to the idea of bringing in more refugees and demonstrating that Canada is there to help, had a few more questions." As a result of the November 2015 terrorist attacks in Paris, Arabs, Muslims, and refugees all comingled to produce the trope of dangerousness. One of the outcomes of this danger discourse was the eventual terrorist attack on a Quebec mosque in January 2017 in which 6 Muslim men were murdered and 19 others were injured as they engaged in worship. This act of terrorism was perpetrated by a White male, Alexandre Bissonnette, who was charged with six counts of murder and five counts of attempted murder using a restricted firearm. However, Bissonnette was not charged with any terrorism-related offenses.

Muslims and ethnic minority Canadians are also subjected to a new form of a racist "civilizing mission" through the discourse of multiculturalism that depoliticizes "difference" in culture, thereby obfuscating racialized dimensions of supposedly freedom-based discourses (e.g., women's rights). This project is not unique to Canada but is also present in other Western liberal democracies. Gendered constructions of culture as religion under the rubric of "multiculturalism" have been used to exclude certain symbols and practices under the guise of protection of the "brown woman" as well as a response to the threat of national identity. Bill 60, also known as the Quebec Charter of Values, introduced in 2013 to the Canadian Legislature, is an excellent example of how racism becomes institutionalized under the guise of unity. One impact of the legislation was to ban public sector employees from wearing a hijab, turban, kippa, or other "ostentatious" religious symbols while on the job. The Quebec Charter of Values highlights the rhetoric of multiculturalism and diversity in Canada. It reveals a discourse of diversity within a framework of unity yet at the same time works to erode that very sense of unity among and between diverse groups. It provides a new framework for regulating the terms of belonging in Quebec and relating the charter to the project for national integration.

Accompanying the "multicultural" neoliberal Western democracy is the rise of the security state, raising issues for policing, nationalism, and the racialized individual. The criminalization of color becomes another way of legitimizing the state. The interaction between racism, law, and crime cannot be underestimated. There is a clear relationship between discourses of security, race/racialization, and the historically specific production and regulation of "foreignness." The security state has grouped ordinary Canadians into political stereotypes and has labeled them as threats, and so it is necessary to analyze how contemporary neoliberal reforms are woven through and shape contemporary racial inequality in Canadian society.[7]

In the decades following the signing of the *Universal Declaration of Human Rights*, Canada continued to be steeped in the practice of racism. Racial segregation was still enforced, and racist policies related to immigration and dealings with Indigenous peoples formed part of everyday life. The legacy of the deeply entrenched history of racism lingers on. Despite de-legislation, racist laws and practices still persist today. The extent to which racism operates within social services systems is very much evident in practices related to immigration, settlement, the justice system, health, and education. There are many different yet similar ways to conceptualize our present state of affairs. For instance, present-day race relations and racism in Canada can readily be situated within a context of colonialism,[8] and these links are explored in greater detail in Chapter 2. Canada's early history as a nation state is deeply rooted in racism. Race riots, segregated schools, racially based union membership, mass deportations of innocent people, state-sanctioned kidnapping of children, and conscious attempts at cultural genocide all provide rich evidence of Canada's legacy of racism. Given this legacy, racism is undeniably intricately woven into the fabric of Canadian society. Richardson, Richardson and Richardson (2000) suggested that the foundation of Canada is built on racism and that attempts to dismantle such structures are seemingly futile because society continues to invent new ways of oppressing the same people.

Despite the magnitude of historical and contemporary evidence showing Canada's active engagement in the practice of racism, some scholars have argued against Canada's complicity in the practice and perpetuation of racism. For example, in his evaluation of the Canadian parliamentary report recommendations on racism, Anand (1998) highlights its severe limitations in light of its conclusion that racial hatred in Canada is limited to extremist groups marginal to Canadian society. Pushing racism to the margins of society helps to bolster the national identity of Canada as a racially tolerant society and obfuscates the notion of Whiteness that is at the very core of debates about Canadian history, geography, and national identity.

A substantial portion of the scholarship on racism in Canada has dealt with the operation of racism through the law and criminal justice system. Backhouse's (1999) legal history of racism in Canada from 1900 to 1950, Mosher's (1998) report on systematic racism in Ontario's legal and criminal justice systems from 1892 to 1961, and Chan and Chunn's (2014) discussion of criminalization of racial minority groups and the racialization of the Canadian criminal justice system contribute to the foundation of this scholarship. Other scholars, such as Jakubowski (1997) and Thornhill (2008), discuss the ideological functioning of the law and its capacity to legitimate the illegitimate (i.e., racism) and how knowledge of the historical complicity and duplicity between law and racism constitutes a precondition for understanding the material reality of racism today.

Change in the Legal Arena

Prior to World War II, questions had been emerging in limited ways in the intellectual and political arenas of Canadian society that challenged the assumptions of legalized discrimination by race, which was so commonplace. However, the structure of the Canadian legal system and judiciary limited the possibility of domestic change. It was in 1949, one year after Canada signed the *Universal Declaration of Human Rights*, that the possibility of legal change began when the final court of appeal for the Canadian judicial process shifted from the British Privy Council to the Supreme Court of Canada. With this shift, a renewed emphasis on the quality of judicial appointments and the importance of an independent judiciary in the legal processes of the country were affirmed. As the Canadian judiciary grew in strength and capacity, it was able to begin the long, slow road toward legal change which would then set the framework for the possibility of a nation that might imagine the possibility of a world standing up beyond the suffocating weight of racism.

The most significant shift in the legal mechanisms of the country took place in 1982 when the Canadian Constitution was patriated to Canada from Britain. The new Constitution enshrined the Canadian Charter of Rights and Freedoms within it. In Section 1 of the act, the Charter guarantees "the rights and freedoms set out in it subject only to such reasonable limits prescribed by law as can be demonstrably justified in a free and democratic society."

In Section 15, equality rights are proscribed as follows:

> Every individual is equal before and under the law and has the right to the equal protection and equal benefit of the law without discrimination, and in particular, without discrimination based on race, national or ethnic origin, colour, religion, sex, age, or mental or physical disability.

With these words, every Canadian is given protection through the Constitution of their rights. No new law can be made that violates the commitment of the Constitution, and existing laws must be interpreted in conformity with this protection.

Of course, the legal and judiciary system remains a human and fallible system. Many lawyers and judges lack education in the area of history, race theory, and awareness that equips them to interpret, apply, and make new law that builds up the intention of the Constitution with regard to its fundamental aims in this area. However, in the movement toward a society less determined by the mechanisms of race and racialized discourse, the Constitution with the Charter remain the strongest ally of change.

The commitment of Canada to move beyond legalized racism, although significant, is fraught with complexity. As noted previously, personal and systemic racism persists. Limitations in our judicial system that allow space for the possibility of racism remain. Two important examples of this lie in the concept of challenge for cause and the practice of peremptory challenges in jury selection. Whereas the criminal code makes provision for challenge for cause on the basis of racial bias of potential jurors in criminal cases, there is no such ability in civil cases. This leaves plaintiffs or defendants susceptible to racial bias in jury composition with the potential for unjust outcomes. In a criminal trial, counsel are allowed peremptory challenges, which means they can reject any potential juror without explanation. The system of peremptory challenges as currently configured means that jury composition can reflect racializing agendas without question. The dominance of "Whiteness" as a category that influences and shapes dominant culture means that in remaining unconscious of the ways racism affects us and may be at work in our systems, the possibility of justice becomes much more elusive. The importance of justice not only being done but also being seen to be done is as manifest as ever.

Colten Boushie

In February 2018, Gordon Stanley was acquitted on murder charges in relation to Colten Boushie of the Red Pheasant First Nation in Saskatchewan. The facts of the case are deeply disturbing. Colton Boushie was shot in the back of the head by Gordon Stanley after Boushie and a group of his friends trespassed on Stanley's property. Boushie was asleep in the car when his friends drove onto the property with the apparent intent of stealing an ATV. Two of his friends, including the driver, fled the scene. It was Boushie who was shot by Stanley. Stanley argued that the weapon misfired and that he had not intended to kill Boushie. Stanley's lawyers exercised their peremptory challenges to ensure an all white jury. The jury returned a verdict of not guilty. There is no guarantee that a jury of a different racial composition would necessarily have delivered a different verdict. However, the use of the peremptory challenges in this way has created the possibility of injustice, both real and perceived.

> **BOX I.I**
>
> ## *A Case of Everyday Racism*
>
> As a professor in a community in which the racialized population is estimated to be approximately 20%, there is often only one or two racialized students in any given year in the program in which I teach. As a racialized professor myself, this fact creates some unique challenges. One evening while sitting in my office, I noticed a student in the hallway. This student had been having some challenges, it seemed, because she was not submitting assignments and not communicating about her academic lateness. I called out to the student, asking her to come into my office. During our conversation, the student noted that she had not been communicating with me because she finds me intimidating and unapproachable. I really wanted to get at the heart of these perceptions of me held by the student, so I probed further, asking what it is that makes me "unapproachable and intimidating." The student replied that I was "tall and fit with a dry sense of humor that was more acceptable in males." Probing further, I drew the student's attention to another professor across the hall from me and asked if she also found that professor to be intimidating and unapproachable because that professor was taller than I am and "fitter" (read skinnier) than I am. The student replied, "No, but you also have to remember that you are Black." The student then went on to note that "I am not racist, I lived in the Caribbean for 2 years."
>
> As the semester progressed and students began to get letters of acceptance into graduate programs, a student approached me to tell of her exchange with another student. The student who approached me was the only Black student in the program that year. She was accepted into a graduate program and was quite excited to share this news with her classmates. One of her classmates, however, commented to her that the only reason why she got into that program was because she was Black. Obviously offended by such a statement, the student objected and was further told that the statement was not meant to be offensive but, rather, to highlight the fact that she (the Black student) was a credit to her race, and she should be proud.
>
> Further on in the semester, a second student approached me to tell me of an incident that occurred in the classroom while completing some evaluation forms. On that day, she forgot her reading glasses at home, so filling the forms out took longer than usual. The student collecting the forms noted, "You're not finished yet? Oh I forgot you are ESL [English as a Second Language]."

> Interpreting the previous two events as overtly racist, I asked the two students if they were comfortable identifying who made such comments only to discover that it was the same student who found me to be intimidating. I asked the students to individually discuss their experiences with the Director of the school because although the incidents were disconnected, they created a pattern of racist behavior that should not be tolerated, especially in a school of social work. I also discussed my experience with the Director, situating it in a pattern of behavior. After meeting with the two students, the Director determined that the behavior of the student who made the comments was "overtly racist" and asked the student to apologize to the two students...and that was that—until it was time for my annual performance review.
>
> During my review, the Dean raised this issue as one that was troubling, noting that the student's family members were donors to the university and they brought to the attention of the Advancement Office that this student was being targeted by me. Citing grades as the issue, it was reported that I was being unfair to the student. I reiterated my position that I followed all the departmental policies related to grading this student and in fact the policies note that after 7 days, the professor reserves the right to not accept any work that is late. This student's work was 41 days late, even after three e-mails from me to the student asking for her work. A late penalty was deducted from the student's submission after grading her work. The student later graduated from the program on the Dean's honor roll as well as with a scholarship.

Questions have been raised as to whether the expressed commitment to multiculturalism as a way of expressing statehood is in fact viable at all. If a nation state is in fact a multinational state, is it anything at all? Apart from questions of national identity, however, are the more pressing questions of quality of life (Box 1.1). These are insider questions: How shall we live on the inside of a world that purports to value equality and dignity beyond any external categories of difference? Canada has chosen for itself a social imaginary whereby we eschew the racialized hegemony of a dominant class in favor of one that shares power through respect for difference as a matter of law and practice. The intention of this book is to move the discourse forward, understanding that an anti-racist perspective and its reception and application are an indispensable pathway for that conversation.

Anti-Racism

The anti-racist perspective is a direct entry point that does not conflate racism with any other forms of oppression. Dei (2007b) posited that there are three conceptual components of anti-racist theory. First, that race is salient and central, not an exclusive social relational category. By keeping race salient and central, anti-racism draws attention to the implicit biases in societal constructions and creates a parallel discourse that makes race relevant in various social interactions. The saliency of race becomes even more critical in a society such as ours, in which a post-racial discourse that depoliticizes race forms part of the societal imagining.

An anti-racist framework also moves beyond an acknowledgment of social structures of inequality to a critical interrogation of Whiteness. Without such an interrogation, Whiteness remains unproblematic and racism will continue to thrive.[9] Whiteness works through processes of normalization by silently imposing itself as the standard by which social difference is to be known. The normalizing of Whiteness is often the difference between criminalization and social supports. As such, a racialized person engaged in criminal activity is readily ascribed labels such as terrorist or criminal, yet Whites engaging in the same activity are more likely to be labeled as mentally ill and constructed as an anomaly to the White standard. Such tendencies of normalization within the dominant culture hide the fact that White is also a racialized identity.

Another defining feature of anti-racism is an acknowledgment of the situational and contextual variations in intensities of oppression and relative saliencies of different identities. As noted by Dei (2007a), it is possible to adhere to the notion of "intersecting oppressions" and "interlocking systems of oppression" and at the same time recognize the persistence and saliency of particular oppressions at given moments in history. Although the politics of anti-racist theory calls for the saliency of race, it does not dismiss the intersections with gender, class, disability, and so on. Furthermore, discourses about the intersectionality of social difference (race, class, gender, sexuality, disability, etc. as linked, intersected, and integrated) must also not lose sight of such differences as sites of marginality and resistance. It is important to stress and hang on to the notion of saliency and the relative saliencies of different identities and oppressions.

> *Intersectionality* is the belief that oppressions are interlinked and cannot be solved in isolation.

While documenting the history of anti-Black racism in Canada, scholars also pay attention to various forms of anti-racism organizing and resisting, including that of African Canadian women in nursing (Calliste, 1996), the development of Black Power groups in Montreal (Austin, 2007), strategies developed by Black Francophones to gain access to power structures (Madibbo, 2006), and the specific contributions of the Black press (Thompson, 2015).

An excellent starting point, if not the primary starting point, in addressing this issue is giving voice to our experiences as racialized people in Canada. We cannot begin to right a wrong, or grieve a loss, or mend a system, without first acknowledging the wrong that has been done, the loss that has occurred and the system that is broken. There has not been an era free of the taint of racism in the Canadian story. A critical step toward change is acknowledging Canada's part and continuing role in the perpetuation and maintenance of racist structures.

In overt but mostly covert and insidious ways, racism and discrimination impact every aspect of racialized immigrant women's functioning in the Canadian space. Its long history and insidious nature complicate strategies of eradication. Although legislation against racism has had measured success in the past, creating a greater level of awareness and sensitivity toward racist actions and thought, such legislation has also had the negative effect of making racism a covert activity and thereby more difficult to identify and address. In many senses, legislation further victimizes the victims of racism; as a result, creating further legislation may not necessarily be the path toward resolution. The inherent difficulty in attempting to address racism in Canada lies in its invisibility. What we can see, we can respond to. As long as we cannot see the racialized Other, we will build our empires on top of her.

Resistance creates new dynamics. So disturbing to White complacency has racism become that there is now slippage in reference to it as the "R" word. The "R" word is a threat to White sensibilities leading to the rise of conditions such as White fragility. The discomfort of race that gives place to this fragility needs to be disentangled from the need to address the race problem. White fragility, otherwise determined as the resultant stress experienced by a White person when called upon to address racist behavior (DiAngelo, 2011), is part and parcel of the politics of racism in which the oppressed become responsible for the oppressors' feelings and Whiteness is once again centralized and normalized. This discomfort of constructively engaging with racism ensures that conversations about race are derailed and the White hegemonic status quo is maintained.

The effects of racism and anti-racism endeavors on racialized bodies are not benign and can be seen across multiple levels of individual and societal functioning. One of the social impacts of racism is the challenge it presents to truly belonging and "occupying" space. In the face of racism, racialized bodies forever feel like cultural outsiders. The fact of racism and anti-racism endeavors creates a state of hypervigilance for racialized people. Both racism and anti-racism are positions of hypervigilance that do not readily allow for the racialized Other to comfortably occupy the space they occupy, thereby heightening a sense of unbelonging. They find themselves not in a transformative space but, rather, in an oppositional one. Anti-racism erects structures of opposition in the face of systemic racism but does not advance the cause for achieving a sense of belonging. Although an anti-racist stance is a necessary one in fighting against and dismantling systemic barriers in part through raising awareness, alone it does not create a safe and comfortable space for belonging and becoming. For that, more is required. For that, a new social imaginary built on the bones of courage and consciousness is prerequisite.

Given the inherent challenges with racism and anti-racism, how then do we keep the centrality of race but create a space in which racialized bodies can belong—a space that moves beyond the discourse of tolerance and inclusion? What seems to be necessary is a radical shift from racism through anti-racism to a space of non-racism viewing such movement as on a continuum. Anti-racism is not a destination but, rather, a resting place along the journey. Standing only as a theoretical construction, a non-racist position, while acknowledging difference, ascribes no value to such differences. Within this construction of non-racism, the oppressiveness of Whiteness, a core component of racism in Euro-descent culture and a central feature of anti-racist work, is addressed.

Prisoner Scream

I scream
I scream so loud; I scream so long
I've lost my voice.
Voiceless, I scream.
I scream inside, no one hears
No one hears
I lay here beneath the weight
Stifling, crying, moaning
Someone passes by
A moment of silent anticipation
Could it be?
There is hope....
The moment's gone
And I scream
I scream again
Voiceless once more
Yet I scream
—Kathy Hogarth

2
What's Post About Colonialism

COLONIALISM IS A relational reality—an encounter between people and a process of conquest and domination through which power relations are inscribed with colonizer on top and colonized under. Although often spoken of as a thing of the past, colonialism is a modern-day, presently occurring phenomenon firmly embedded from our history and entrenched in our present. There is nothing post about colonialism! In this chapter, we examine post-colonial discourse and discuss particular ways in which continuing faces of colonialism challenge the notion of post-colonialism. We consider the ways in which the colonial mind is reinvented in everyday practices and policies and use case examples to illustrate such reproductions. The central thesis of this chapter is that the legacy of colonialism continues to operate through various forms of reproductions in a "post-colonial" era and that such reproductions of colonialism continue to be evident in the unequal relationships between racialized Others and the "rest" and between First and Third World nations and the political and cultural interdependence of subjugated bodies. In this chapter, we lay out a historical sketch of colonialism, examining the various ways in which colonialism was practiced in Canada from pre-contact, moving from the Royal Proclamation of 1763 to the implementation of Bill C-31 in 1985. Furthermore, we examine the various forms of reproductions and renegotiations evident in scholarship, practice, and policies and how these reproductions continue to impact and shape the lives of colonial Others in Western spaces.

Two key terms are elucidated further in this chapter. We adopt a more Marxian view of colonialism as a form of capitalism, enforcing exploitation and social change for largely economic reasons. From this perspective within the global capitalist system, colonialism is closely associated with uneven development through means of dependency and systematic exploitation, inevitably producing distorted economies, sociopsychological disorientation, massive poverty, and neo-colonial dependency. As it relates to scholarship, we draw attention to how White ventriloquism has dominated Western feminism in such a way that it has silenced the voices of racialized people and served as a mechanism of further oppression. Furthermore, we demonstrate the flow of scholarship between the West and the rest and how this flow serves as a mechanism of maintaining hegemonic relationships between subjects and masters.

Canada and Colonization in Historical Perspective

Before we can apply the concept of post-colonialism, then, we have to grasp the meaning of the project of colonization and the colonial intent in the Canadian context as our beginning place. The necessary vehicle for that is an exploration of what colonization looked like and what was intended in the story of the legacy of the British Empire in Canada, with particular reference to Indigenous persons. It is to that story that we now turn.

Through the hearings held in support of the Truth and Reconciliation Commission in Canada, witnesses talked of an experience of having been used in a variety of experiments during their time in residential schools. The data to support and illuminate this contention, beyond the memory of now adult children, have been sparse. However, as research has continued, new dimensions of the residential school experience have emerge.

In a paper published by the *Social History Journal* in 2013, historian Ian Mosby documented the story of various nutritional experiments conducted in Canada between 1942 and 1952 involving Aboriginal communities and residential schools. Within this time period, during World War II, nutrition experts from various departments of the federal government wanted to explore the relationship between malnutrition and general health issues in Indigenous populations.

An early report during the study hypothesized in 1942 a connection between rampant tuberculosis (TB) and poor diet. A death rate from TB of 1,300 per 100,000 was documented in Manitoba, compared to 27.1 per 100,000 for the non-Aboriginal population in the same province. As well, the overall death rate in the province was five times higher than that in the non-Aboriginal population, and the infant mortality rate was eight times higher. It was the connection between hunger and malnutrition and other health issues that the interested researchers wanted to explore.

Toward that end, an intensive 1- to 2-year study was proposed to be conducted on "a limited number of Indians," which would study the effects of selective interventions on the observed populations. This goal set in motion a series of studies involving several Indigenous communities that unfolded over a decade. The forms of the experimentation were diverse.

By 1942, because it was known that children in the residential schools were starkly undernourished as a baseline, government groups began to study the population. Between 1948 and 1953, the Department of Indian Affairs (DIA) performed a series of experiments involving more than 1,000 students in six residential schools throughout the country that documented the effects of various vitamin interventions (including increased milk consumption and the use of vitamin-enriched flour) and increased food provision (caloric intake) compared to control groups that remained undernourished, as well as the impact of fluoride on teeth and dental care.

Within broader Indigenous communities, through strategies such as surveys conducted at Norway House, Cross Lake and James Bay, the dietary impact on health of forced and selected food consumption was explored. This was achieved through the implementation of controls of family allowances. Government regulations were put in place that controlled the types of food that Aboriginal families could purchase in government stores with their subsistence allowances, as a vehicle for measuring the impact of consumptions of certain foods on health.

Using human beings as subjects in forced nutritional experimentation with unknown consequences to health and well-being is a disturbing reflection of a Canada that existed prior to contemporary norms related to the ethics of research involving human subjects. More disturbing is the racialized discourse that allowed these subjects to be Indigenous communities and children. When the studies began in 1942, the perceived negative character traits of the Indigenous person were assumed. However, even as they were postulated as normative, it was hoped that nutritional research might find some potentially correctable link between nutrition and perceived moral defects. In 1942, initial findings from an experiment with 300 Indigenous persons were reported as follows (Tisdall & Kruse, 1942):

> It is not unlikely that many characteristics, such as shiftlessness, indolence, improvidence and inertia, so long regarded as inherent or hereditary traits in the Indian race may, at the root, be really manifestations of malnutrition. Furthermore, it is highly probable that their great susceptibility to many diseases, paramount amongst them tuberculosis, may be directly attributable to their high degree of malnutrition arising from lack of proper foods.

With this report, we observe the extent to which Aboriginal persons and their worlds were objectified and made the subjective data of hegemonizing pseudo-scientific inquiry through forced and often unwitting participation in a social engineering experimentation, which had disastrous consequences for their physical as well as emotional well-being. The justification for this was the assumed racialized discourse of Canadian society.[1]

First Nations and Colonization in Canada

British interest in the land mass that would become known as Canada gathered momentum in the last half of the 18th century. Britain and France had been contesting for global dominance in a variety of arenas, one of which was North America. By 1763, France's interests in North America had been soundly defeated, and the British king planted the flag of his empire firmly in the soil in areas previously held by the French.

When Britain declared British North America a colony, many persons already lived there. Some of those were descendants of French immigrants from prior generations, but much more numerous were a variety of First Nations persons from many tribes and cultures who had inhabited the land for at least 10,000 years prior. Although there is no undebated theory as to how and when Aboriginal peoples first occupied this territory, the most broadly regarded theory is that varieties of peoples made their way across the Bearing Strait at least 12,000 years ago. The number of tribal groups present in "Canada" at the point of contact with the British is not known. However, even after generations of forced assimilation and loss of tribal groups through disease and other challenges, currently there are 53 distinct language groups within Canada that have survived, with 11 language families. This remnant reflects what is understood to be a large and broad diversity of cultures already inhabiting the region.

When the British began their relationship with First Nations communities, they elaborated a clear commitment to a policy of "Friendship," with Indigenous persons guaranteed the right to self-government. This policy was announced with the British Royal Proclamation of 1763. The British government wanted to befriend native peoples and to respect their right to carry on with their ways of life, as prior to British contact. The principles that would govern this policy of friendship were laid out in the Proclamation, including the principles by which formal agreements between the Crown and First Nations communities known as treaties would be developed. Treaties were formal agreements that usually implied the relinquishment of land to the government in return for certain monetary or other values. The general view of an aspiring post-colonial hermeneutic is that many of these treaties, rather than serving as documents that equally protected the interests of both parties, favored Crown interests and exploited First Nations interests. Most treaties were written between 1701 (French era) and 1923. Note that not all treaties were regarded as unfavorable by Indigenous communities, but the general principle of treaty making was a colonial strategy designed to protect the interests of the colonizer in the first instance.

The policy over the course of the 100 years leading up to Confederation (Canadian nationhood) in 1867 changed rapidly. The policy of friendship was replaced first by the idea of civilization and then, by the time of Confederation, with a government commitment to the total assimilation of First Nations peoples (see Milloy, 1998, pp. 6–21).

How did this shift occur in the mind and policies of the colonizer? The answer to this question is primarily economic, with emergent racism serving as a justification. As discussed in Chapter 1, the idea of race was new in the emergent modern era, and it gained currency as a mechanism for marginalization and domination as the economic activity of 19th-century colonialism expanded. In other words, as more European immigration created the demand for more space, primarily good agricultural space, the government adopted policy directions that would allow the forced migration of Aboriginal peoples off of their traditional territory into marginal spaces where Europeans did not want to live. Forced migration was allowed by emergent government policy that named Indigenous person as "uncivilized." Dominant European culture and English language (with the Francophone exception) were defined as normative. As a matter of law, Aboriginal languages, cultures, and ceremonies were defined first as inferior and later as intolerable.

With the introduction of the Gradual Civilization Act of 1857, the British Colonial government introduced the idea that Indian persons should be "civilized" and retrained to resemble their Anglo neighbors. It was theorized that this process of civilization would take place through education. If an Indian person agreed to be re-educated in the form of an English person—adopting Anglo language, culture practices, and renouncing all claims to tribal status—then at that point he would join Canadian society proper and be allowed the rights of an adult person (i.e., an adult male person because women of any racial group were not enfranchised in British North America at that time). If, on the other hand, an Indian person did not follow this civilizing path, then he was declared effectively a ward of the state, along with all tribal groups in emergent Canadian society. The Canadian government in the form of the Department of Indian Affairs (variously named throughout the years) served the function of in loco parentis setting up a system of paternalistic control that would limit the capacity of Indigenous communities to self-actualize and enshrined their marginalization within the social geography of Canada for all of its history to date.

By the time Canada started its life as an independent nation (1867), the policy of civilization had shifted to an overt policy of assimilation. It was agreed by the body politic through its first parliament that the total eradication of tribal groups through cultural assimilation was required for the future of the new nation. Assimilation was to be achieved primarily through education but also through the legislative regulation of every aspect of Indian life, including the criminalization of Indigenous culture as discussed later; the forced removal of Indigenous persons from their land when treaties or other agreements could not be negotiated; and the limitation of Indian persons including freedom of movement and lifestyle, consumption of alcohol, and all other basic human rights generally acknowledged as the entitlement of Canadian citizens, such as the right to vote in elections, choose how to educate one's children, and so on. The legislative commitment to assimilation was sealed in 1869, with a revision to the 1857 Gradual Civilization Act, signed by Sir John A. MacDonald, Canada's first prime minister, which officially revoked Aboriginal self-government. This action of course undid the commitments of the Royal Proclamation of 1763, which had guaranteed self-government and the commitment to relate to First Nations tribal groups as distinct nations.

Broad Limitations of the Indian Act

The Indian Act is the principal statute through which the federal government to this day administers Indian status, local First Nations governments, and the management of reserve land and communal monies. It was first introduced in 1876 as a consolidation of previous colonial ordinances, including the Gradual Civilization Act of 1857. Its purpose, as with other government policies related to Indigenous persons, was the complete assimilation of Canadian Aboriginal communities. The act has restricted the rights and freedoms of Indigenous peoples in many ways, including the following: the creation of reserve lands and residential school (both discussed later); restriction of First Nations persons from leaving reserves without express permission of the government-appointed official known as the Indian Agent; the enforced enfranchisement of any First Nations person admitted to university (loss of tribal status);

expropriation of reserve lands for public uses, up to and including moving an entire reserve without prior consent of the community; leasing uncultivated reserve lands for agricultural purposes to non-Indigenous farmers without consent of the band council; prohibition of the sale of alcohol and arms; imposition of the band council system; forbiddance of the practice of traditional Indigenous religion; prohibition of all First Nations people from appearing in any public event wearing traditional regalia; criminalization of the potlatch and other cultural ceremonies; and denial of the right to vote.

It is the case that many of the previously mentioned provisions were removed from the act approximately a century after their imposition. However, the act, which is still enforced, holds sway over much of Indigenous life in Canada in a way that limits rights and freedoms of whole nations of people.

Criminalization of Indigenous Culture

True assimilation could only be attained through the abolishment, by law, of all cultural practices. Hence, under the Indian Act (an updated version of the Gradual Civilization Act of 1857), the Potlatch Law, which included other ceremonies such as the Sun Dance, came into effect in 1880. Section 3 of An Act Further to Amend the Indian Act, 1880, made the exercise of these practices a criminal offense.[2] Depending on the culture, potlatch ceremonies could, for example, be held to celebrate the passing of names, titles, and responsibilities of one chief to the eldest heir; distribute wealth; establish rank; mark the passing of a chief or the head of a house; or celebrate weddings and births. Recognized as integral to the culture of coastal First Nations, the potlatch was targeted with particular force. The government viewed potlatch ceremonies as barriers to assimilation and as such criminalized them as a necessary dimension of cultural eradication and successful integration of the Indian into the body politic of Canada.

Reserve Lands: An Exercise in Containment and Control

Reserves in the Canadian story are analogous to the homelands of the apartheid era in South Africa. In fact, after the conclusion of World War II, South African officials visited Canada's DIA to explore how Canada was managing and containing its "Indian problem." The apartheid system that was subsequently developed in South Africa took the idea of separation onto segregated land for whole tribal groups from the Canadian practice. The Apartheid system was dismantled in 1994, whereas the Canadian reserve system remains in effect to date.

Under the Indian Act, an "Indian Reserve" is land held by the Crown "for the use and benefit of the respective bands for which they were set apart" under treaties or other agreements.[3] Many First Nations (Indian bands) include several separate portions of land as their reserve. Only those with Registered Indian status (i.e., Status Indians) may "own" land on a reserve, although such ownership remains at the discretion of the Minister for Aboriginal Affairs and Northern Development and does not entail full legal possession. Certificates of Possession, often referred to as CPs, convey "ownership" of reserve lands to their holders, but they lack the legal status of deeds. In other words, the land given in treaties was not given with right of ownership analogous to Euro-descent Canadians. Control of the land to this day legally remains the preserve of the colonizing interest—the Canadian government.

Education as an Assimilationist Tool

The Indian Act was adapted in the 1880s to make the provision for residential schools as a requisite educational model. How did this infamous chapter in Canadian history begin? As the new Canada began its life, it understood Aboriginal persons to be a problem. Frequently in government communications, there is reference to the "Indian problem." Seeking a response to this problem led to the creation of a commission known as the Davin Commission. Its task was to study the Indian problem and make a recommendation as to the best solution, with a view to setting up industrial schools (residential training schools) rather than day schools for the education of Indian children. The Davin Commission met for almost a decade, submitting its report in 1879. The major finding of the report was that the total assimilation of the Indian into the Canadian body politic was the desired goal and that this could best be achieved through education.

The Davin Commission consulted the Bureau of Indian Affairs in the United States, which had previously begun a boarding school model of education while simultaneously maintaining a military action against Native Americans on the western frontier. Economic analysis showed that it was cheaper to educate an Indian than kill one, and as such the educational model of assimilation was to be preferred.

The Davin Commission recommended the development of schools consistent with the American model, which was one built on a church-government partnership. In this partnership, the government set policies, inspected the schools, and provided per capita funding. Perhaps most important was the recommendation that attendance at the schools be compulsory, replacing day schools as a potentially more effective vehicle for assimilation.[4] This recommendation would lead to the policy that allowed the forced removal of all Indigenous children aged 7 years or older from their parents.

Some parents relinquished their children willingly. Others did not. When the schools first opened in 1890 and 1891, less than 20% of all Indigenous children registered in DIA schools were in residential schools; the remainder attended day school and were able to return to their homes in the evenings. When the next series of management agreements were signed in 1911 between governments and churches, more than 78% of all Indian children registered in schools were in boarding schools, with only 22% in day schools.

Perhaps the most distressing aspect of this story is that when the new management agreements were signed in 1911, it was known that the residential school model was not working. The Canadian government underfunded the schools, trying to run them on a more cost-effective basis than their American counterparts. This led to all manner of local suffering for the children who were placed in the schools. Decade after decade, reports surfaced that rang the alarm bell as to the horrific conditions in the schools. In 1907, Chief Medical Officer for the DIA Peter Bryce wrote a report that documented the high rate of illness and death in the schools. Bryce was so alarmed by what he found that he called for a Parliamentary inquiry into the condition of the 72 schools then in existence. No inquiry was held. Instead, in 1911, the new agreements were signed, with one significant attendant policy change that referenced the age at which children could be seized from their parents for placement in the schools. Stressing that "we must take the children younger if we are to have any hope of defeating the influence of the wigwam," the government lowered the minimum age of children for the schools from 7 to 4 years (Bryce, 1922).

Conditions in the schools included poor levels of education, inadequate nutrition, dilapidated and unsafe buildings, and poor supervision leading to abuse of all kinds. During the depression, the DIA cut funding for the schools by a further $840,000. During World War II, further budget cuts to the schools were undertaken. Underfunding of the schools may have been the single most significant factor in determining the extensive level of suffering children experienced in the schools. The implications of this are further explored in the micro-narrative, a case study of the Mohawk Institute residential school, later in this chapter.

In 1948, Canada became one of the original signatories to the United Nations' *Universal Declaration of Human Rights*. Along with many other nations, Canada affirmed the following:

- Everyone has the right to life, liberty and the security of person (Article 3).
- No one shall be subjected to torture or to cruel, inhumane, or degrading treatment or punishment (Article 5).
- Everyone has the right to a standard of living adequate for the health and well-being of himself and his family, including food, clothing, housing, medical care, and necessary social services; education shall be directed to the full development of the human personality and the strengthening of a respect for human rights and fundamental freedoms; parents have a prior right to choose the kind of education that shall be given to their children (Article 25).[5]

Unfortunately, back at home, Canada continued with its Indian Act in effect and residential schools in full force. That the country did not recognize the dissonance between what it said it believed and how it lived with reference to its racialized policies against First Nations peoples is one of the greatest tragedies in Canadian history.

Things did slowly begin to change. After 1949, the DIA started to reflect on the possibility of closing the residential schools. That conversation went on for 20 years. In 1969, the policy to close the schools was adopted by the liberal government of the day. Although most of the schools were then closed in a matter of several years, particular circumstances meant that there were a few remaining schools into the 21st century. Currently, all residential schools are closed.

In 1951, Section 149 of the Criminal Code was repealed, which meant the ban on Indian ceremonies was dropped federally. Provincial legislation on this matter remained in effect for many years longer in some places. In 1960, only 5 years before African Americans were given the right to vote in the United States, voting rights were extended unconditionally to First Nations people.

In 1985, the Canadian government passed Bill C-31. With this bill, important changes were made to the Indian Act, bringing it into line with the provisions of the Canadian Charter of Rights and Freedoms. The three principles that guided the amendments to the act were removal of discrimination based on race, religion, and gender; restoration of Indian status and tribal membership rights; and increasing control of Indian bands over their own affairs.

These changes were all positive steps in moving away from the racialized oppression against First Nations peoples that began in the 19th century. However, they are incomplete. The Indian Act, with many problematic limitations of the rights and freedoms of First Nation's people, remains. The capacity for self-government is largely denied. The reserve system remains in place, and living conditions on many reserves are well below the national standard for even basic necessities of life. Some of the realities of existence for Indigenous peoples in Canada include the fact that many First Nations children never graduate from high school and most never attain a post-secondary education. In fact, secondary school data identify the rate of First Nation graduation at approximately 36% (and lower in some regions of the country) compared to the Canadian graduation rate of 72%, and only 4 in 10 young adults living on reserves throughout the country have finished high school.[6] Clean drinking water has been and remains a threat to the well-being of Indigenous peoples on reserves. Currently, approximately 73% of First Nations water systems are at high or medium risk of contamination. Rates of addiction are far above those of the general population, and rates of suicide among First Nations youth are much higher than the national average. Rates of employment on reserves are dismally low because many reserves have no ability to provide employment for their young. Approximately 50% of all children who are seized by Canadian Children and Family Services are Aboriginal, and First Nations men are the largest group of persons imprisoned in the Canadian penal system, with Indigenous women currently the fastest growing sector of new incarcerations. In some prisons, more than 50% of the prison population is Indigenous. In Manitoba, that figure is 71% (Fraser Report, 2014). The fastest growing category of persons incarcerated in Canada is Indigenous women.

These realities of Indigenous people's existence in Canada reflect the legacy of colonization that is alive and continuing to harm one sector of Canadian society simply because of these people's racialized identities. Coming to consciousness about this and moving beyond the dominant culture is the challenge that this book lays down.

The social historian knows that narrative and its meaning are played out most deeply at the level of everyday experience. It was at the level of everyday experience that the meaning of this colonial discourse of dehumanization played itself out. What was the everyday experience of children who were raised over several generations in residential schools? What does the content of the experience say about the lived meaning of an assimilationist monologue? The Mohawk Institute (MI) was the longest lived residential school in Canada. Built by a missionary society known as the New England Company in 1832 at the Six Nations Reserve in Brantford, Ontario, it housed Indigenous children until 1971. For each of the generations it stood, children knew various experiences of dehumanization, violence, humiliation, nutritional deprivations, illness, lack of medical and dental care, substandard education, and sometimes untimely death (Box 2.1).

For decades, students experienced various forms of deprivation while at the school. The adequacy of children's clothing persisted as a constant refrain through the decades of our narrative. In 1939, an anonymous writer sent a letter to the DIA reporting that it was well known in Brantford that the children were not adequately clothed. The letter noted that it was then November and "the boys are still without underwear. They only received stockings one month ago. Light cotton clothes are worn summer and winter. Even the poor clothes they have are often dirty and ragged."[7] The Brantford League of

---

BOX 2.1

The Case of Wilhemina Hill

Wilhemina Hill was 4 or 5 years old (the school staff did not know for sure) and a student at the MI in 1934, when she contracted TB. Wilhemina's number was 01059. Because she had been assessed as being tubercular, she could not stay at the MI. She could not go home because her mother had died and there was no other alternate supervision. Snell wanted to send her to the Sanitarium in Brantford but could not do this without authorization from the DIA because the cost for her to live at the Sanitarium was $1 per day. The DIA Secretary in Ottawa, Mr. Mackenzie, did not agree to pay the $1 per day. He asked the DIA-appointed physician, Dr. Davies, to assess the situation. Dr. Davies confirmed the diagnosis and recommendation. However, the government refused to authorize the extra money (which was considerably more than the per capita allowance it paid for her to live at the MI). The correspondence went back and forth.[a] Wilhemina died at the MI before any authorization was given for the transfer. Several other students contracted TB. False economy? Obviously, the value of an Indigenous child's life was limited in the ethical system of the assimilationist monologue.

a. Letters and telegrams from Snell to MacKenzie and also to and from Dr. Davies, from July 4, 1934, to July 30, 1934; RG 10, Volume 6202, file 466-13, part 1.

Christian Women found in 1946 that children were underfed and that inadequate food made it particularly concerning that there was no regular medical or dental care for the children at the MI.[8] In the late 1940s, the same league of women expressed concern that children were not provided with socks, winter coats, or boots in the middle of southwestern Ontario winters.[9] No one listened. Well into the 1950s, the question of providing adequate clothing with the limited DIA allowance for provision was still at issue. The school principal, John Zimmerman, insisted that if the point of a residential school education was to prepare children to become part of dominant culture, then they must be dressed as White children are dressed.[10] The quality of education at the MI was often under critique. Underfunding by the government meant that for most of the MI's history, teachers who would work for less or who could not find work elsewhere were hired, and usually there was an inadequate number of available teachers. The curriculum taught at that time was partly academic and partly industrial. Students spent half their day in the classroom and half engaged in manual labor designed to "train" them for service work employment. In this program development, we witness the intersection of the race, gender, class triangle that was so embedded in the colonial project. Boys were trained according to the gender assumptions of maleness and girls for domestic labor for the same reasons. Both boys and girls were trained for manual labor related to gender roles—not to serve as future professionals but as future servants. This reflects, then, the class assumptions that permeated the residential school project. Boys worked on the MI farm, and girls worked in the kitchen, laundry, and as seamstresses and housekeepers. Girls were also sent off the property to work as servants in some wealthy Brantford homes for which the school received a stipend. This off-site work often ended in complications for young girls who returned to the MI pregnant at the hands of those in whose homes the girls worked.[11] The combined education/work model of education together with the small number of teachers meant that an MI education during that period often left students barely literate.

Consistent underfunding by the government affected the quality of life that children enjoyed outside of the classroom. It meant that there was inadequate after-school and night-time supervision of children, including inadequate supervision of recreation, which led to peer oppression and, occasionally, accidental death (Box 2.2).

Throughout the period under consideration here, the MI was inspected, monitored, and assessed by many government offices. By 1960, in addition to the DIA, several other bodies were involved in monitoring and supporting the work of the MI, including the Children's Aid Society, the local Mental

> ## BOX 2.2
>
> ### *The Case of Effie Smith*
>
> Effie was a 13-year-old girl living at the MI when she died in 1936. The school lacked playground equipment. For many years, there was a hand-made toy known as the May Pole. The May Pole was an automobile wheel on a shaft adapted to fit at the top of a pole. The device was used to swing around, as in the traditional May Pole dance. Children often used this device unsupervised. Throughout the years, the May Pole was used variously, sometimes as a form of peer punishment. Unpopular children were strapped by the arms to the device and swung round and round until they vomited.[a] The day Effie died, there were no adults supervising the play. Apparently, the wood broke away on one side of the pole, causing it to fall, and Effie was crushed in the midriff. She died of internal hemorrhaging at the scene of the accident. There was an inquest, and the finding was for accidental death. Proper playground equipment, maintenance, and play supervision were recommended. The mother of the child did not blame the school but in fact requested a spot for her younger son in her daughter's place.[b] Funding to increase supervision of the children was not forthcoming.
>
> a. Internal school memo; RG 10, Volume 8605, file 451/1-13, part 1.
> b. *Brantford Expositor,* May 16, 1936, and letter from Snell to the secretary of the DIA, May 25, 1936; RG 10, Volume 6200, file 466-1, part 2.

Health Clinic, the National Health and Welfare Service, a Brant Public School inspector, Superintendent of Schools Regional Office, and Six Nations Inspectorate of Schools. We see that from the beginning, the MI, as with other residential schools, became a warehouse, intended for assimilation of the children of the racialized Other. However, even with the extremity of the schools, the project of racialized assimilation ultimately failed. Canada's commitment to pursuing the hegemony of a racialized normativity, however, was ingloriously enshrined.

What began as bilateral discourse in the context of friendship in 1763 ended as an assimilationist monologue—the language of hegemonic discourse. The residential school experiment was designed to build the new nation of Canada through re-creating Indigenous persons in the image of the dominant Euro-descent culture. Rather than promoting enfranchisement and nurturing democracy, Canadians saw the fabric of their basic convictions cut away as the experiment in social engineering became a human rights nightmare. Throughout, the basic assumption that indigenous children were somehow less than others was used to justify government underfunding and what amounted to callous disregard for human suffering. At the level of social history, the meaning of opting into a model of confluence characterized by an assumption of racial superiority and justifiable dominance is clear: It did not work. Paradoxically, in fact, it took Canadians away from the primary project named as democratic humanization, toward dehumanization and loss of national soul.

Colonial Reproductions: The Methods of Reinvention

The notion of "post" colonialism is a highly debatable one. As noted by Loomba (2015), the prefix "post" erroneously complicates issues because it assumes an end to colonialism despite evidence of ongoing inequalities between the previously colonized and colonizing nations. The identities of post-colonial bodies are often deeply forged through their experiences with their colonizers. Failure to recognize the continuation of colonialism, and thereby framing Western societies as post-colonial, not only perpetuates the myth of post-colonialism but also sets a stage for continued atrocities within those spaces.

The production of stereotypical and antithetical knowledge that often compares "the Other" (read undesirable) against the West (read desirable) is a strategy by which colonial discourse gets its authority and is being used to regulate, discipline and keep the colonized "Other" in "their" debased place (Chakrabarti, 2012; Hamadi, 2014; Said, 1978). Here, we examine further particular ways in which colonialism continues to be reproduced specifically through domestic and international policies, academia, practice, and feminist discourse.

Canadian Policies

Not all Canadians are created equal with regard to health and wellness. In his award-winning book, *Clearing the Plains: Disease, Politics of Starvation, and the Loss of Aboriginal Life*, medical historian James Daschuk (2013) explores how racism among policymakers and the general Canadian population serves as a key factor in the poor health outcomes among First Nations communities. This relationship is a historic one that persists to the present day.

Daschuk (2013) explores the *politics of famine*. He argues that if the Canadian government had acted in good faith with its treaty obligations, the spread of epidemics and starvation would have been limited. However, he further argues that the withholding of nutrition and medical care facilitated the endgame of the government, which was ultimately the eradication of Indigenous peoples. Attempts by First Nations communities to resist and advocate for fair treatment fell on deaf ears. Each passing decade of the 19th century brought a new dimension to the impress of subjugation on Indigenous communities, including such things as the building of the Canada Pacific Railroad, repression of uprisings, starvation, and untreated TB. By the time residential schools were implemented in 1891, the landscape of social disaster had been fully defined. The schools were designed to serve as the final suite of the assimilation *opus*.

As we consider policies, it is of utmost importance that we take hold of a central principle of colonial functioning that governs both the past and the present. This principle simply is that policies were designed to best serve the needs of the colonial master and not the needs of colonial subjects. One of the most vivid examples of this is how policies were used to manage Indigenous and Black people in opposing ways to meet the needs of the settler colonialists (the elimination of the Indigenous people and the capture and containment of the slave). Through the "one drop rule," the whitest of Blacks was bound to slavery because the policy ensured that the offspring of a slave and any other parent with any African ancestry, no matter the distance and regardless of the physical characteristics or appearance, were enslaved, thereby increasing the number of slaves who could serve the colonists' interests. The opposite was true for Indigenous people. Whereas one drop of Black blood forever tied Blacks to the land as slaves, one drop of White blood forever separated the Indian from the land as Indigenous. The Indian was a problem to be dealt with by subtractive measures, and therefore the most Indian of Whites lost status as an Indian. This restrictive racial classification of "Indians" played a crucial role in the logic of elimination.[12] The fewer the number of Indians, the fewer the number of claims to lands. Over subsequent generations, the reduction of Indigenous claims to land would allow for a corresponding increase in settlers' claims to land and property.

Stepping forward from the time of first colonial encounter, we are able to see the grip of colonialism with the introduction of Indian residential schools. These schools were introduced with the aim of educating, civilizing, Christianizing, and ultimately assimilating Aboriginal people into Canadian society (Aboriginal Healing Foundation, 2005). The first Indian residential school in Canada opened in 1831, and the last federally run Indian residential school closed in 1996. During that span of time, it was estimated, although no accurate count of the total number of students is available, that in excess of 150,000 Aboriginal children were separated from their families and communities (Aboriginal Affairs and Northern Development Canada, 2008). Many suffered emotional, physical, and sexual abuse, and others died while attending these schools.[13]

In 2008, Prime Minister Stephen Harper made a statement of apology on behalf of Canadians for the Indian residential school system. In his apology, Prime Minister Harper noted that "there is no place in Canada for the attitudes that inspired the Indian Residential Schools system to ever prevail again." However, if "killing the Indian in the child" was the strategy of eradication and domination when Indian residential schools were first introduced, despite the end of residential schools, the strategy of eradication and domination is still in effect.[14]

Canadian child welfare policies are skewed in such a way that they allow for a gross overrepresentation of Aboriginal children in care.[15] The Sixties Scoop was a phase in Canadian history during which there was a mass removal of Aboriginal children from their homes, who were then placed into the child welfare system. The Sixties Scoop has been overtaken by what some refer to as the Millennium Scoop.[16] A Statistics Canada (2013b) report showed that in 2011, Aboriginal children accounted for nearly half (48.1%) of all children in care in Canada, even though Indigenous persons represented less than 2% of the Canadian population. This disproportionate representation of Aboriginal children in care, although not very well understood,[17] has at least two derivatives tied to colonialism: a reinvention of colonial mechanisms and a legacy of colonialism.

Arguably, as agents of the state, child welfare authorities are continuing to advance the state agenda of eliminating the "Indian problem." The majority of Aboriginal children in care are placed with non-Aboriginal foster parents; thus, opportunities for transferring Indigenous cultures and ways of knowing and being are bleak. This crisis of care for Aboriginal children inevitably leads to the bolstering of Eurocentric values and the elimination of Indigenous culture. The imposition of Euro-Western legislation and the ongoing marginalization of Indigenous knowledge continue to undermine attempts made within Aboriginal communities to stem the tide of Aboriginal children being placed in non-Aboriginal homes.[18]

Apart from colonial reinventions as evidenced through the child welfare system, Aboriginal communities are living with the legacy of colonialism in a highly magnified way. Despite Canada being rated as one of the best countries in the world in which to live,[19] levels of poverty in Aboriginal communities are a stark reminder of the negative impacts colonialism has had on societies. Recent research shows that at least 50% of Aboriginal children in Canada live in poverty,[20] and as noted by Macdonald and Wilson (2013), "a 50% poverty rate is unlike any other poverty rate for any other disadvantaged group in the country, by a long shot the worst".[21] Poverty and poverty-related issues such as poor health, massive unemployment, and poor living conditions are a blight on First Nations communities throughout Canada. These issues can be directly linked to the economic driver of colonialism. Aboriginal peoples and communities had their own economic and cultural systems intimately linked to the lands they inhabited. Removed from their lands, their capacity to be economically self-sufficient was taken away. Poverty cannot be divorced from the loss of traditional lands. The land was a central mechanism of the vibrancy of Aboriginal communities—not only as a means of physically sustenance but also as a means of sustaining their culture and heritage. One of the atrocities of colonialism and its continuing reinvention is the continuing encroaching of Aboriginal lands. Unresolved land disputes are likely to be in the Canadian courts for generations to come.

Assimilationist strategies have been aimed not only at Canada's Aboriginal population but also at any group viewed as different or deviating from the Canadian norm. More recently in Canada's history, the theme "immigrants assimilate or go home" has been loudly proclaimed throughout Canada. In 2011, the government of Canada issued a ministerial order to ban face coverings—another of many direct attacks on Muslim identity in Canada. Much of the public discourse around the issue of the niqab has little to do with the fact of what women are wearing and much more to do with the fact that the niqab is a marker of a failure to assimilate to Canadian culture. In 2013, the Quebec government introduced Bill 60, also known as the Quebec Charter of Values. The bill sought to impose conformity, particularly related to religious neutrality but ultimately infringing on the fundamental freedoms of those who hold to practices and traditions that are different from the norm.

Another of the multiple ways of reproducing colonialism is seen in Canada's immigration policy. The development of immigration policy parallels Canada's policies of assimilation. A history of Canadian immigration from the point of Confederation in 1867 and the subsequent Immigration Acts of 1869, 1919, 1952, and 1967 until present unearths a well-established pattern of domination and control for the economic advancement of a nation. Despite the first Immigration Act of 1869 having a theoretically explicit "open door" policy, as discussed in Chapter 3, this aspect of the policy did not translate into practice until the early 1880s when Chinese labor was deemed necessary for the building of the Canadian Pacific Railroad. This open vision was of course conditional: Once the building of the railroad was completed, the Chinese Head Tax was imposed in 1885, effectively slowing the pace of arrival of new Chinese.

An often ignored element of global migration and the policies that support it is the havoc it reaps on developing countries. Immigration policies in the West consistently appear self-serving: They continue to facilitate the mining of skills and educated talent from "Third World" and developing countries. The scale of this "brain drain" is startling. Data show that nearly 1 in 10 tertiary-educated adults born in the developing world now live in the developed world (Lowell, Findlay, & Stewart, 2004). This movement of human capital from developing countries to the developed world has a profoundly negative impact on source countries.[22]

As is the case for many other countries in the Global North, Canada's immigration policy facilitates in great measure the ongoing mining of skills and education from developing countries. Amendments to the 1967 Immigration Act specifically targeted immigrants who would make the greatest contribution to Canada. The amendments resulted in a points system in which immigrants were awarded the greatest number of points based on their education level—the more educated the immigrant before arriving in Canada, the more desirable he or she was.[23] The latest changes to the selection system in the Immigration Act were introduced in 2002, with the new system being even more heavily weighted toward formal education of applicants.[24] Although building a strong population base may in and of itself be blameless, failure to take account of the impact of such policies on a global balance of opportunity and capacity reflects a neo-colonial lens. The inevitable result of this kind of mining is the brain drain that continues to undermine the development of capacity in countries of the Global South, leaving them once again in a "one down" position at the global table.

Although net impact, which takes into consideration factors such as remittances, inward investments, and charitable activities of diaspora, may often show some positive effects of the phenomenon of brain drain,[25] even after accounting for these potentially positive aspects of "talent migration," developing countries are still negatively affected.[26] In immigration discourse, much is spoken of in terms of the benefits of immigration to Canada. Conversely, little is ever said about how the gains to Canada impact the home countries of immigrants. If one holds a narrow nationalist view, this approach to immigration may be arguable. However, as citizens of a global community with a vision for a more livable world for all, this approach to who gets in and who does not perpetuates an imbalance reminiscent of the colonization game from earlier times.

Academia and the Colonial Mission of Enlightenment

According to Said (1984), colonial education is the "process or policy of establishing and maintaining an empire lingering where it has always been, in the general cultural sphere as well as in specific political ideological and social practices" (p. 9). This "empire lingering" is reflected and accentuated in Western forms of education as the academy engages in multiple modes of exploitation and colonial reinvention. In fact, from the very start of the modern colonial project, education was one of the stated goals along with the mission of "Enlightenment" for those outside the Euro-descent veil. There are two clear paths of reinvention in the academy that are explored here, namely how it is reflected in the production of scholarship and how the academy serves as a driver for notions of cultural competency.

One of the clear ways we see the continuing grip of colonialism is in the institutional culture of the academy that continues to privilege Whiteness and Anglo-Eurocentric ways of knowing. Colonial education reinforces Western knowledge and ways of life as the epitome of knowing, at the expense of the traditional knowledge of other societies, thereby creating a desire in the colonized to aspire to see and be a part of Western society. Education was used as a mechanism of control during the colonial era to normalize the Westerner's ways of life. Colonial education also caused deep spiritual and mental scars in the colonized "Other," leading to their mental and physical enslavement. Without a mental "decolonizing," the physical trappings of colonialism continue to maintain their power. Gaining political and economic control of a people is achieved in tandem with mental control, and as demonstrated with the residential school project, that is what colonial education did. It created a way for the colonizers to control the colonized mentally, by leaving out and systematically devaluing the multiplicity of preexistent knowledges in the "New World," including Indigenous ways of knowing. Wane (2006) suggested that to control people's culture and way of thinking is to control how they define themselves in relationships with others. She stated that the education currently available in the colonized nations is a form of colonization in and of itself because it continues to instill in the people the beliefs and cultural symbols that portrays the West as a superior and more desirable "Other," while similar elements of preexisting rich and diverse cultures are missing from the curriculum. The continuing loss of language among so many Indigenous groups in the Americas is a painful illustration of this point. This act confirms our fear that colonialism did not end when the colonizers "left" colonized societies to repair themselves. In fact, there is validity in the question, Did the colonizers actually leave or did they simply replicate? Colonialism is still ongoing through the education system and through other organizations or institutions that are only now beginning to raise the question of what it means to make space for Other wisdoms in critical social spaces.

One very demonstrable way of assessing the academy's continued colonial empire building is through the flow of scholarship. Very little, if any, scholarship enters into the "First World" space from Second or Third Worlds.[27] What we see instead is a unidirectional proliferation of "First World" literature and scholarship dominating the academy in other worlds, thereby enshrining colonial ways of knowing as absolute and disprivileging other ways of knowing with a trickle, if any, scholarship from Third and Second Worlds entering the First World academic space. Herein lies the challenge of emancipation from mental slavery when education is a "good" master and the only choices laid before one is to educate or remain "uneducated." This very dilemma confronted Indigenous elders in the 19th century when they were forced to choose between educating their children in the White man's way and losing their Indigenous heritage or risking annihilation as peoples—quite literally.

Despite this ongoing reach of colonial education, the academy at the same time contributes to the ontology of forgetting and erasing Canada's history of colonialism and racism. A paradox exists in the academy today. To work in the world of Western higher education, one must be conversant in the idea of "diversity." However, the acquisition of skill in this area begins from the presumption of normativity—by which Western ways of knowing are the spine and all else is the "diversity." The emergence of cultural competency as a tool for managing and understanding diversity, first in the classroom and then extrapolated to practice settings, as such becomes quite problematic as a colonial reinvention. The argument that notions of cultural competency provide us with the supposed ability to interact effectively with people of different cultural backgrounds in fact resembles a new form of racism by Othering non-Whites and deploying modernist and absolutist views of culture while not using racialist language, but instead using culture as exclusionary.[28] Cultural competency views culture as neutral and devoid of power and therefore does not theorize power or critique systems of oppression, let alone analyze the role of Whiteness in academia. Whiteness is the default color standard from which racial minorities are evaluated and often found to be lacking in some respect.

In academia, notions of cultural competency inform disciplines far and wide, and this is particularly true of disciplines with direct interface with the general public. The argument made for cultural competency is as a means of addressing the ever-growing cultural diversity of the West, and as a result, both educational and professional standards in many of these disciplines have incorporated cultural competency as a major feature. Medicine,[29] social work, public health, sociology, and business,[30] to name but a few, have all incorporated cultural competency in their ritual practice of education. In its position statement on cultural competency, the Canadian Nursing Association noted that educators have the responsibility for "promoting cultural competence within the faculty and the student populations."[31] The notion that one *can* gain cultural competence through a course or degree, or short practice experience, models the arrogance of the neo-colonial mind. The notion that one *should* perhaps more so.

Using the profession of social work as an example, we are able to gain a glimpse into how academia becomes complicit in maintaining and reinventing colonial power relations with cultural competency as a driver. The colonial code still informs much of social work's professional values and how those get translated into practice. Several social work scholars have examined how the ongoing discourse of cultural competency in social work eclipses race as a central mechanism of oppression and reinforces a "color-blind" lens (Razack & Jeffery, 2002; Schiele, 2007; Yee, 2005). In addition, these scholars note the limitations of adopting a cultural competency framework because such a focus at an individual level does not prepare social workers to address institutional racism and oppression at all the other levels of operation (Pollack, 2004; Potocky, 1997). The model of cultural competency promoted in social work reduces issues of racism to an individual level, thereby enshrining systemic issues. In addition, we argue that the very thought that one can become competent in another's culture is, in and of itself, a colonial regression.

Western Feminist Discourse as a Colonial Marker

Feminist theories evolved as a way of explaining pervasive gender inequalities. B. Smith (1991) stated that feminism is the political theory and practice that struggles to free all women: women of color, working-class women, poor women, disabled women, lesbians, old women—as well as White, economically privileged, heterosexual women. Anything less than this vision of total freedom is not feminism, but merely female self-aggrandizement. (p. 106)

In feminist theories, gender difference is central. The differentiation of human beings based on their gender is a significant factor affecting practically every aspect of our daily lives.

Despite the vision of "freedom," Western feminism provides us with another clear example of colonial reproduction. Tied up in feminist discourse is the politics of representation, or who speaks for whom, and who produces knowledge about whom. This notion of representation remains a major problem in feminist research. White ventriloquism has dominated Western feminism in such a way that it has silenced the voices of racialized women and served as a mechanism of further oppression. Western feminism in this regard has become the colonizer of women of the Two-Thirds World. Ganguly (1995) highlighted this issue, noting that it is "particularly pertinent in the case of women from minority backgrounds who have so often seen knowledge of them constructed for the purposes of reinforcing stereotypes and controlling them" (p. 5).

Another major concern related to the politics of representation in feminist discourse is the universalizing of women's experiences. The projection of White women's voice on the rest has created a form of "ethnocentric universalism" that Mohanty (1991) characterized as a mode of structural domination that suppresses the heterogeneity of "Other" women. This ethnocentric focus of Western feminism does not take into account the unique experiences of women from Third World countries or the existence of feminisms Indigenous to Third World countries, nor does it take into account indigene feminism. One, and not by any means the only, element missing from Western feminist discourse is how race is intertwined with gender and that responses to gender are often informed by experiences of race and vice versa. The voices of women from the Two-Thirds World are not the same as the voices from the Western world. Too often the one has silenced the "Other."

Arguing against the discursive colonization of Western feminism and highlighting the need for a Third World feminist approach, Mohanty (2003) noted that assumptions of privilege and ethnocentric universality, on the one hand, and inadequate self-consciousness about the effect of Western scholarship on the Third World in the context of a world system dominated by the West, on the other, characterize a sizable extent of Western feminist work on women in the Third World. (p. 19)

Similarly, Hawkesworth (2006), quoting the Association of African Women for Research and Development, noted,

While patriarchal views and structures oppress women all over the world, women are also members of classes and countries that dominate others and enjoy privileges in terms of access to resources. Hence, contrary to the best intentions of "sisterhood," not all women share identical interests. (p. 124)

Monolithic nature of Western forms of feminism often negates complex social hierarchies embedded within the concerns and interests of women from different regions, classes, cultures, nationalities, and ethnic backgrounds. Although there is a universality in gender subordination, feminism must take into consideration the individuality of women's experiences. Absorbed in the politics of representation, Western feminists replicate patterns of Western hegemony, exercising influence beyond their geographic and national borders, selectively permeating the boundaries of other nation states and other women's lives. Being conscious of the significant dangers that varieties of cultural essentialism pose to feminist agendas, Uma Narayan (2000) suggested that the

development of a feminist perspective that is committed to anti-essentialism both about "women" and about "cultures" is an urgent and important task for a postcolonial feminist perspective. Such a perspective must distinguish and extricate feminist projects of attending to differences among women from problematically essentialist colonial and postcolonial understandings of "cultural difference" between Western culture and its "Others." (p. 91)

Although there are marked similarities between Western feminism and Third World feminism, Narayan (1997) highlighted one of the distinctive features. She noted that "a critical understanding of the 'cultural distinctions' constructed in colonial struggles is salient to contemporary Third World feminist agendas" (p. 14). According to Mohanty (1991), women in the Third World believe that Western feminism bases its understanding of women on "internal racism, classism and homophobia" (p. 49). As a result, Western feminism shows its limitation in its understanding of Third World and post-colonial women.

The post-colonial feminist perspective emerged from the gendered history of colonialism and engages in direct critique of Western forms of feminism and their universalization of female experience. Mills (1998) depicted post-colonial feminists as feminists who have reacted against both universalizing tendencies in Western feminist thought and a lack of attention to gender issues in mainstream post-colonial thought. One of the critical arguments of post-colonial feminists is that cultures impacted by colonialism are often vastly different and should be treated as such.

Post-colonial feminists such as Gayatri Spivak (1999), Chandra Mohanty (1991), and bell hooks (2000) are critical of Western forms of feminism, objecting to the portrayal of women of non-Western societies as passive and voiceless victims and the portrayal of Western women as modern, educated, and empowered. These portrayals further entrench systemic oppression relating to the colonial experience, particularly racial, class, and ethnic oppression, and continue to marginalize women in post-colonial societies.

Conclusion

Common understandings of colonialism are engaged with notions of settlement of bodies in new locations. These understandings, although holding great truth, are very limited and lacking in depth of analysis. Whereas some elements of colonialism revolve around the settlement of bodies, other significant dimensions of colonialism revolve around geographical space, and both are inherently tied to issues of power and domination. Colonialism is a relational reality—an encounter between people and a process of conquest and domination through which lives are forever changed.

The undying legacy of colonialism serves both as a connector and divide in two very significant ways. On the one hand, it provides a bridge and a chasm between those who claim and occupy "First World" space and those in various Third World nations in a series of complicated and unequal relationships. On the other hand, it connects and divides those who occupy the mainstream space from Others in their *own* societies whose unequal relationships to the mainstream are themselves products of Western colonial history. Although often spoken of as an era gone by, or a thing of the past, the reality is that colonialism is a modern-day, currently occurring phenomenon firmly embedded in our history and even more so present in our everyday lives. There is nothing post about colonialism! Instead, the era of so-called "post-colonialism" signals unfinished business and the continuing collective struggle of colonized bodies for their own redemption. Neo-colonialism seems a more true account of our present state of functioning. Colonial masters have changed, and colonial bodies are ever evolving.

Despite so-called "gains" to the colonized,[32] colonialism, its continuing legacy and reinventions, has had a dominant pattern of dependency, systematic exploitation, and the reification of power. Colonialism then and now leads to the same outcome with the ultimate result being the uneven development of cultures and societies. The colonial generated cultural disruption not only reifies power but also, in so doing, reifies dependency and creates a sense of sociopsychological disorientation.[33]

Token Ism

I am a token
Moved here and there in the game of ism
Chosen as a prize, rejected as a flaw
Passed on, skipped over
I am a token.
Knocked over, picked up, strategically placed
Opposing, disposing
No token wins in this game of ism
Don't hate the token, hate the game
Whose turn is it?
Vanquish the isms, vanquish the token
Game over

—Kathy Hogarth

3

Belonging and Diaspora

WHAT DOES THE story in Box 3.1 have to do with diaspora and belonging? If nothing else, it speaks to how as Others we come to negotiate belonging in spaces of difference. As diasporic peoples, this negotiating of belonging is both personal and political, and it is highly charged with issues of race, class, and gender. Our engagement within and without the diaspora is tempered by our experiences personally, professionally, and politically. There is a necessary blurring of the boundaries between the personal and professional, between the micro and the macro, which must occur as we attempt to understand issues of diaspora and belonging.

We live in an increasingly interconnected and globalized world. National economies are linked worldwide, and information can be transmitted throughout the world in mere seconds. In this process of transnational expansion, the very definition of what constitutes a nation and nationalism in many areas of the world has been expanded to include individuals from different countries and, more important, members of ethno-racial communities. But crossing boundaries is not a new phenomenon as the world has always been affected by transnational forces. Although the concept of transnationalism has been widely used across disciplines, and therefore variously defined, it generally refers to "the multiple processes" that allow people to live in ways that span two or more societies simultaneously, essentially merging these multiple locations into a single field of activity. The concept of transnationalism raises issues of diaspora and belonging that are worthy of consideration. Diaspora, in particular, has acquired new meanings related to notions such as global deterritorialization, transnational migration, and cultural hybridity. To understand diaspora and belonging, we further need to understand concepts of rootedness, citizenship, and nationhood. How do we understand territory and develop common definitions and understandings of these terms in a way that adequately captures their inherent fluidity?

BOX 3.1
Negotiating Belonging

Whiteness never bothered me—as a matter of fact, neither did Blackness. I existed far beyond the notions of color—that is, until I entered the White space. Then color defined me, and as I was defined, I began to define through the lens of Black and White. I realized that in the White space, color mattered, and at times it seemed to matter much more than anything else I embraced as my identity.

The fact of color seemed to always unsettle my belonging in the White space. As I traversed the geographical borders of White and Black space, my border experiences serve to further unsettle those experiences of not belonging. And it is funny in a not so funny way that when I first entered Canada as a landed immigrant, the reception was so warm and welcoming—it was my most hassle-free experience traveling to another country.

On Mother's Day of 2009, I got a call that my grandma was dying. Up to that point, grandma had not seen my daughter, who at that time had just turned 1 year old. As a matter of fact, with the exception of my mom, none of my family members had seen her beyond photographs. It was important for me and my mom that before my grandma passed away she would get the opportunity to see my daughter. I booked a flight the same day and flew home that evening. I traveled light—two carry-on pieces. I had a great time back home connecting with family, enjoying my sisters and spending time with my grandparents. My grandma was overjoyed. Two days seemed too little, but still I had to leave.

On my return to Canada, I was pulled off the flight when we landed. All I was told at that time was to go to a different section and an officer would be with me. Three hours later, with a highly agitated baby strapped to me, I approached an officer to ask for directions to a bathroom, at which time things took a turn for the worse. I said, from a distance of about 10 feet, "Excuse me." The officer spun around and shouted "Ma'am, please take a seat" and at the same time she grabbed her hip. For a split second, I wondered if she thought the baby strapped in front of me was a weapon of mass destruction because in that instant she responded as though she felt threatened, but I could not understand why. I shouted back at her with matching venom in my voice, "I need to use the bathroom." In the same tone, she said, "An officer will accompany you to the bathroom, take a seat." I was outmatched; I took a seat and waited.

About 45 minutes later, a White male officer approached me and asked if I still needed to use the bathroom. I thought, "Really? I'd rather wet myself than have you accompany me," but I said, "I do but I'd rather know why I am being detained." He stated he was not at liberty to tell me except that I was a person of interest. I asked, "Why? What have I done to make me a person of interest?" I recounted in my mind all the actions I had taken before leaving Trinidad. Preboarding I sat in a secluded area but close to the gate because my daughter was just learning to walk and I wanted her to have unencumbered space. I was preboarded because I had the infant with me. I sat in-flight beside two elderly persons and never once got out of my seat because I did not want to trouble the elderly gentleman in the aisle seat who had kidney troubles. I took my time and exited the flight as I struggled with my baby and two carry-on pieces. What in all of that would make me a person of interest? The officer then pointed to another Black female at a remote end of another room and asked if I knew that person. I said, "No I've never seen her before." He then said, "Well it was made to seem as though you were traveling together." In my mind, something did not sync. How could that be? I don't know how many Black people there were on the flight. I do know there weren't many, but to pull two into detention for me raised that nagging question of the role of color in this experience.

Without explanations, I was left with only my assumptions. These assumptions are about the stereotypes of Black Caribbean women as drug whores. Hence the need for the long waiting period to observe my level of agitation and discomfort. Hence the need for the officer to accompany me to the bathroom and hence the search. Four hours later, after being humiliated, searched, and questioned, I left the Toronto airport. I left with my experience that has traveled with me ever since—an experience, one of many, that has taught me that I am more likely to be targeted because of my color. That my identity in this space is color coded, and those codes often read "suspect," "terrorist," "threat," and "thief." How can I ever hope to belong in this White space that through the gaze of these Black eyes reflects racist, oppressive, and basely brutish?

This chapter starts with laying out traditional conceptualizations of diaspora and the challenges and commonalities associated with forced and voluntary diasporic groups. We engage in a historical elaboration of belonging and diaspora, exploring the experiences of Chinese and Japanese Canadian immigrants from the late 19th to the mid-20th century. We examine how legalized racism affected their movements, location, and social participation, including the forced displacement of the Japanese as a historical case study. We also explore shifting notions of diaspora and particularly how advances in technology impact belonging within these groups. Toward this end, we engage in this chapter with the concept of e-diaspora, giving attention to how migrant belonging is negotiated in a digital age and taking into consideration both assentation and contestations of migrant belonging.

Understanding Diaspora

The documented history of Canada is of course an immigrant story. First Nations peoples alone predate that narrative—everyone else is here as a result of migration in some form. The issue of migration as it was impacted by racialization relates to our work here with regard to (a) the displacement of First Nations persons as discussed in Chapter 2 and (b) as discussed in this chapter, the "management" of the location and inclusion of immigrants as an exercise in hegemonic control by a British colonizing force, later expanded to include an English-speaking Euro-descent ruling social elite.

Our opening premise is that English-speaking, Caucasian peoples were welcomed by the colonizer and settled on favorable lands often through the displacement of Indigenous persons. Our following premise is that as immigration expanded to include persons from other linguistic, cultural, and racial groups, the rate of their migration and their placement in the social imaginary was tightly controlled to construct a racialized vision for what the new Canada should look like.

Space and Social Imaginary

As we attempt to understand and deconstruct the lens of a colonial legacy with regard to the social landscape of race set against the backdrop of class and gender, the work of French philosopher Michel Foucault is helpful. Foucault coined the term *heterotopia*. He developed this idea in reaction to his historical observations about the systems of normativity that have pervaded the development of Western culture and that have served as a vice into which all are directed to fit. The rigidity of social spaces defined by race, class, and gender assumptions has led to the development of laws and worldviews that ensure their replication (Foucault, 1967, 1984). The story we consider here with regard to immigration and migration in Canada supports Foucault's concern.

Discontented to allow the enforced state of hegemonic normativity, Foucault invites the reader to consider space differently. Heterotopia names the phenomenon of a space that is created which is unique, informed by layers of meaning that may not immediately meet the eye. Postulating a duality in space both social and physical, he argues that there are many layers of reality existing in parallel. A heterotopia is a contained and particular universe of meaning shaped by both objective and subjective dimensions. A heterotopia pushes against the binary oppositions of a hegemonic narrative by insisting that competing truths, claims, experiences, and forces frame the discourse of meaning. In this regard, the lived experience of art in relationship fulfills exactly this function. We see the world and define our reality in new ways through encounter with and in the experience of difference. Rather than controlling and segregating difference as we have been inclined to do in Canada, a heterotopic worldview would invite us to deconstruct our old segregations based on race, class, gender, and worldview.

Social geographer Edward Soja took Foucault's concept of heterotopia and from it developed his theory of "Third Space." Soja's argument is that in the experience of Third Space, there is a confluence of realities that create an experience which integrates the known and unknown, the objective and subjective, the abstract and the concrete, mind and body, the universal and the particular, all of which inform consciousness in an "othering" of any knowing. In our discourse of anti-racism as a necessary partner in genuine and effective multiculturalism, we invite the reader to imagine the world that is possible through the creation of Soja's Third Space as a result of embracing the complexity of a world viewed through a heterotopic lens.

In other words, we become strange to ourselves and in so doing find new ways of imagining our own stories and the possibilities in the worlds around us—or we do not. This process, which is intensely personal, becomes then intensely social as our transfiguration becomes the agency of new social imaginaries—or can be used to reify worldviews and embed them as social reality in policy and forms that cast our worldviews into stone. Foucault would argue that much of the history of Western culture has been used in the service of the latter.

As we consider then the matter of diaspora and belonging in Canadian historical discourse, we use the language of space, its use and control. Access to the Canadian experience was controlled: There were only so many spaces for immigrants of particular ethnic and racial categories. The spaces occupied by new immigrants were redefined upon entry into Canada through access: Asian immigrants and Asian Canadians could live only in certain places and work only in certain roles. This reality reflects then a hegemonic use of space as a racial discourse. Our goal in considering this past use of space is to open the possibility of a new social imaginary whereby all spaces—geographic, social, cultural, religious, and economic—are unlimited for all who participate in Canadian society.

Using Foucault's heterotopic lens as a method of analysis of the current state of affairs for diasporic groups in Canada, we can immediately begin to see significant elements of contradiction. One such area of tensions salient to our understanding of diaspora is how discourse is used to effectively create fissures between the Other and the dominant society. The very terms used in the characterization of the Other serve to destabilize, dislocate. For example, the "immigrant" is never and will never be just "Canadian." Even when citizenship is attained, the immigrant becomes a "Canadian citizen" or some other hyphenated derivative that is still distinctly different from "Canadian." There are a number of problems associated with categorizations such as "visible minorities," "immigrants," and "refugees," not the least of which is how they subject racialized bodies to experiences of racism and identify them as less than "Canadian."[1] To this end, race theorist Bannerji (2000) noted that such terms

> encode the "us" and "them" with regard to political and social claims, signifying uprootedness and the pressure of assimilation or core cultural-apprenticeship. The irony compounds when one discovers that all White people, no matter when they immigrate to Canada or as carriers of which European ethnicity, become invisible and hold a dual membership in Canada, while others remain immigrants generations later. (p. 112)

Amid such "othering" discourse, how do racialized bodies and diaspora ever come to belong? How is citizenship to be negotiated? If we adopt a very unnuanced and political view of citizenship, then citizens are deemed to be those who satisfy particular criteria within a prescribed geographical boundary. Borders once served as the defining characteristic of belonging and citizenship. Geographical boundaries were prominent markers of who belonged or did not belong to the nation state. However, much of that has changed given mass migrations and the transatlantic movement of persons.

The geographical borders became permeable. Nonetheless, where the geographical barriers vanished, political, legal, and social barriers were erected. Belonging and citizenship became and remain a highly contested issue.[2]

The act of citizenship only captures the legal and political aspects of belonging; it does not adequately address the social elements of belonging. In his book *Community: Seeking Safety in an Insecure World,* Bauman (2001) countered the notion of homogeneous belonging. He suggested that

> none of the groups [to] which we enter do we belong "fully": There are parts of our modular persons which "stick out" and cannot be absorbed nor accommodated by any single group, but which connect and interact with other modules. (p. 161)

From this perspective, the migrant body will never "fully" belong but remains in an in-between state of belonging and not belonging.

Immigration and Other Laws Defining Space by Race

Attempting to measure the way in which race reflected and defined Canadian society through a consideration of its laws is complex. As previously discussed with reference to First Nations persons, as a matter of law, place and participation were circumscribed and managed through the Department of Indian Affairs. With other racial groups, the matter is less clear-cut but also demonstrable.

The first Canadian census of the 20th century was taken in 1901. In it, racial designations were defined for census takers as follows:

> The races of men will be designated by the use of "W" for white, "R" for red, "B" for black and "Y" for yellow: The whites are of course the Caucasian race, the reds the American Indian, the blacks the African or Negro and the yellows are the Mongolian, Japanese and Chinese. But only the pure white races will be classed as whites. The children begotten of marriages between whites and any one of the other races will be classed as red, black, yellow, as the case may be, irrespective of the degree of colour.[3]

The census categories notwithstanding, the term *race* is variously used as a legal category between 1900 and 1950. However, laws grounded in the limitation of access, place, and participation by racial group did exist. As well, immigration laws through acts of Parliament were set in relation to racial and national categories: Immigration laws blatantly blocked entry by race, in an effort to protect the "overwhelming whiteness" of the population (Backhouse, 1999, p. 247). The right to vote was explicitly tied as a matter of law to race, with Indigenous Canadians, Chinese, Japanese, Hindu, and "Mongolian and other Asiatics" receiving enfranchisement at different points in the 20th century. As well, inversely we can observe that in the 1930s and 1940s, there was some shift in the application of race in social hegemonizing, as legislators began to enact statutes to prohibit racial and religious discrimination in the insurance industry, in social welfare programs, in the labor movement, and in land transactions (p. 281). With those actions, we see that the systemic practice of racial limitation was at work in key sectors of Canadian society prior to the initiated change. How long it took to change social practice after legislative change is another question entirely.

The Lens

The early 20th century saw immigration into Canada in many forms and in several waves. Between 1890 and 1910, the gross national product increased by 122% due in large measure to the global economic expansion of the British Empire. Canada was a significant provider of raw materials, and much of the lumber that went into the British ships that would carry imperial expansion originated there. Prime Minister Wilfred Laurier announced that the 20th century would be "Canada's century."[4] A deluge of settlers arrived after the turn of the century. In 1896, less than 17,000 immigrants entered Canada. In 1901, 50,000 came. In 1906, more than 200,000 arrived. Between 1901 and 1911, more than 1 million persons from Europe made their way to the Prairie Provinces alone as new immigrants. The vast majority of this immigration was limited to immigration from the United States, Britain and Eastern Europe. However, there were exceptions to this, as discussed later.

With regard to the huge influx of immigration, the agenda of the Canadian administration was highly assimilationist. As with First Nations peoples, all newcomers were expected to conform to a Western model of normativity. The churches, particularly the Protestant churches, became significant agents of this assimilation project for new immigrants, as they were with Indigenous children.

Social activist J. S. Woodworth provided an interesting lens on this phenomenon with his book *Strangers Within Our Gates*, published in 1909. With this text, Woodsworth framed the immigration question as both a world problem and a matter of Canadian identity. Because so many immigrants were arriving in the young nation from so many different places of origin, he puzzled over the issue of the impact of a large number of "strangers" when Canada's identity was still nascent.

Woodsworth's (1909) perspective was comparatively positive for his day. However, his work categorized all groups of immigrants and articulated common stereotypes by racial and national groups. Expressing concern about the way in which the Orientals were "swamping" British Columbia, he opined that the Chinese bring with them "transplanted heathenism" (p. 104). He worried about the Japanese, who were taking over the fishing industry in British Columbia (BC), "now almost entirely in the hands of little brown men" (p. 182). He expressed distress over the "Hindu problem," noting that BC had attempted to limit their immigration into the province through the introduction of the Natal Act, which set an educational test for entrance, prior British military service notwithstanding. Noting the failure of the act to stem the tide, he wrote, "The uneasiness of the people of British Columbia, face to face with the possibility of the hordes of the Indian Empire swarming in upon them can readily be imagined" (p. 188).

Woodsworth was known as a leader in innovative social policy within the new Canada. His view of immigration and its potentially negative impact on the Canadian social fabric demonstrates the embedded nature of assumptions about race and value. Prior to his work as a politician, Woodsworth was a Methodist missionary. His views reflected the strong linkage between religion and the politics of the day. His work ends as an appeal to the Christian Protestant churches to convert Catholics from Eastern Europe, Jews from everywhere, and Buddhists, Hindus, and Sikhs from the Orient to Protestant Christianity as a vehicle not only for their salvation but also for their effective assimilation into Canadian society, which he and others of his day defined as normatively White, English speaking, and Protestant (Woodsworth, 1909, p. 108). The only positive outcome for newcomers was full assimilation into a Caucasian Euro-descent normativity, even as such assimilation was the only place imaginable for First Nations persons in the social imaginary.

The Chinese Experience

Chinese immigration to Canada began in approximately 1858 in response to what was known as the "Gold Rush" in British Columbia. Of course, Canada was not yet a nation, and what would become the province of British

Columbia did not join Confederation until 1871. In 1858, people from many areas throughout the world flooded into the BC region to try to make their fortune in the hunt for gold in the Fraser Valley region. Most Chinese immigration, however, occurred in support of the gold rush, with workers arriving to build roads and provide other infrastructure support labor for the enterprise. The gold frenzy had largely died out by the late 1860s. Chinese workers who had come to Canada became the target of local hostilities because they were perceived to be taking jobs (employment spaces) from Caucasians.

It was not until there was a new need for cheap and exploitable labor that Chinese immigration was again encouraged. In 1881, construction of the national railway (Canadian National Railway) had begun. Given the desire for low cost and the brutal conditions under which the railway would be built, Chinese immigrants (predominantly males without families) were allowed into the country. Between 1881 and 1884, more than 15,000 Chinese came to Canada, of which 6,500 were employed directly by the Canadian Pacific Railway and the rest were largely employed by ancillary businesses in support of the railway initiative. Given the harsh working conditions, it is estimated that at least 600 persons died during the construction of the railway, but no one is certain of the death toll. In regions, local communities refused to allow the burial of the Chinese dead in Christian cemeteries. First Nations communities were known to have opened up their burial grounds to welcome these strangers who passed, when others would not.

Upon completion of the railway in 1885, Canada moved to once again limit the immigration of Chinese to Canada. The Canadian parliament passed the Act to Restrict and Regulate Chinese Immigration into Canada. This act introduced a "head tax" of $50. The idea behind the head tax was that potential Chinese immigrants would be discouraged through an inability to pay the tax. No other immigrant group was targeted this way.

The Canadian government was discouraged to find that the imposition of a head tax did not stem the flow of Chinese immigration. As such, it took measures to increase the tax. In 1900, the head tax was raised to $100 per person. In 1903, it was raised again to $500 per person. Through this process, the Canadian government raised more than $23 million from Chinese immigration.

Meanwhile, anti-Asian sentiment was running high in Canada, particularly on the West Coast. Although government immigration policy specifically legislated against Chinese, within the society as a whole, this distinction tended not to be as clear. As Japanese workers migrated from California to Canada on the heels of an economic slowdown in the United States, fears among White workers grew and there was a violent outbreak of vandalism, harassment and assault in Vancouver's Chinatown and Japantown. Canadian legislators responded by working to further limit Asian immigration into Canada and participation in both the workplace and society, particularly for the Chinese.

In 1912, the intersection of race, class, and gender occurred in a unique legal construct that limited the place and participation of White women as a vehicle for limiting the scope of Asian economic activity. The "White Woman's Labour Law" was first enacted to prevent the employment of female labor in certain capacities (Backhouse, 1999):

> No person shall employ in any capacity a white woman or girl or permit any white woman or girl to reside or lodge in or to work save as a bona fide customer in a public apartment thereof only, to frequent any restaurant, laundry or other place of business or amusement owned, kept or managed by any Japanese, Chinaman or other Oriental person. (p. 136)

In 1917 and 1918, provincial legislators in Ontario, Manitoba, Saskatchewan, and British Columbia passed similar laws making it illegal to hire White women to work in Asian-owned businesses and restaurants. The perceived need for this legislation indicates that (a) new Asian Canadians were successfully developing businesses and making a place for themselves in their new country despite resistance and (b) Euro-descent Canadians were working through the vehicles of social power available to them (law) to circumscribe and limit Asian Canadians while also reinforcing a social hierarchy of race, class, and gender. This workplace legislation took racial ideologies to new heights. In the United States, there was legislation that prohibited intermarriage between White women and Asian males but no law as extreme as Canadian law (e.g., limiting work). With this law, the Canadians made their first declaration of "Whiteness" as a legal category in law (Backhouse, 1999, p. 137).

Meanwhile, despite government efforts at population control through immigration law, and social control through workplace regulation, the Chinese population continued to grow. According to a report of the Methodist Missionary Society, in 1919, there were 6,000 Chinese persons in Vancouver with 210 families, and in Toronto there were 2,100 Chinese persons with 35 families.[5] Chinese families, although small in number, were also limited in the social spaces they were allowed to inhabit. In the city of Victoria, BC, several measures were taken to segregate Chinese from the rest of Victorian society. For example, Chinese persons were allowed to sit only in the upper gallery (the balcony) of the Victoria Opera House. They were not allowed to swim in the city's famous "Crystal Swimming Pool," and one store manager limited the hours when Chinese customers could patronize his store—for the "comfort" of his White patrons. Between 1907 and 1921, several efforts were made to segregate the school system for Chinese students even though the number of Chinese families was small. In 1921, the School Board of the City of Victoria successfully passed a by-law segregating schools for Chinese children.[6]

This demographic snapshot shows that the Chinese community in Canada was comprised predominantly of males who came to Canada without their families to establish themselves, with the goal of bringing their families to Canada at a later time. However, the drastically rising head tax made it very difficult for their families to follow them.

The challenge of family reunification became much more extreme in 1923 when the Canadian government passed the infamous Chinese Immigration Act, known as the Exclusion Act. This act prohibited the immigration of Chinese to Canada almost entirely (there was an exception provision if immigration was needed to assist a White man). Ironically, or perhaps symbolically, this act was passed by parliament on Dominion Day (Canada's national holiday). It became known in the Chinese Canadian community as "Humiliation Day," and the community refused to celebrate Canada's national holiday until an apology for the act was given in 2006 by then Prime Minister Stephen Harper.

The Exclusion Act was repealed in 1947. During this period, less than 50 Chinese persons were allowed to immigrate to Canada. This meant that family reunification became an impossibility. The repeal of the act built upon a post-war decision of the provincial government of British Columbia (the province with the largest Chinese population) to give the right to vote to all Asians who were Canadian citizens who had fought in World War II. With the repeal of the act, the story for Chinese in Canada began to shift. Along with this repeal, the federal government gave the right to vote in federal elections to the Chinese. In BC, the provincial government gave the right to vote to all Chinese throughout the province.

The Japanese Experience

Japanese immigration to Canada had not been circumscribed in the same way that the Chinese had experienced—there was no imposition of a head tax. However, quotas negotiated with the Japanese government were in place from the beginning. Immigration from Japan began in 1877, and by 1914 there were 10,000 people of Japanese ancestry living in Canada. Until 1907, as with the Chinese, most immigrants were single men. After the Asian riots of 1907, the Canadian government limited the number of Japanese male immigrants to 400 per year. This meant that most Japanese immigration from that point forward comprised women joining their husbands or unmarried women coming to marry Japanese men already resident in Canada. In 1928, the immigration quota for Japanese was restricted further, limiting the flow to 150 persons in total regardless of gender. All immigration from Japan ceased with the outbreak of World War II and, except for family reunifications, was not resumed until 1960.

As well as enforced limitation on immigration, when Japanese persons arrived in Canada (predominantly into BC), their participation in provincial life was circumscribed by provincial laws and statutes. Japanese were prevented from working in mines—a key economic sector in the province at the time. They were prohibited from participation in provincial and local elections and also prohibited from working in any project funded by provincial government money.

As discussed previously, it is the case that once in Canada, the Japanese were treated in a limiting manner, as were other Asians. However, the full reach of xenophobia with regard to Japanese Canadians was not disclosed until World War II. With the outbreak of war with Japan, Japanese Canadians were perceived as a threat. This perception led the Canadian government to take actions that violated the basic human rights of Japanese Canadians and created a harm that is largely unresolved even today. In response to the attack on Pearl Harbor in 1941, between 1942 and 1949 Japanese Canadians lost their right to live and work as they chose, sparking a redefinition of social space that was more dramatic than anything that had occurred previously in Canada.[7] The movement of 23,000 Japanese Canadians (of which 13,309 were Canadian citizens by birth) during the war years, accompanied by a legislated loss of property, is one of the great harms in the Canadian national story.

In early 1942, William Lyon Mackenzie King, the Prime Minister of Canada, issued a series of Orders-in-Council. These orders allowed the evacuation of all persons of Japanese ancestry from the BC coastline. A 100-mile-wide strip was designated as a protected area. In January 1942, all males between ages 18 and 45 years were removed and taken to the interior to work in road camps. By March of that year, all other persons, including women and children, were instructed that they would also be removed from the 100-mile area. The British Columbia Security Commission began a process of removing all Japanese persons from their homes. This forcible evacuation happened quickly, with no immediate plan for the support of the people involved. All persons were allowed to take only what they could carry with them. Their remaining property was taken into "protective custody." The first 2,500 people were "relocated" to Hastings Park, the site of the Pacific National Exhibition. There, they were housed in the agricultural buildings in the stalls usually designated for animals during exhibition season. Conditions in this makeshift internment camp were terrible, with no proper facilities for sanitation and no privacy.

Eventually, the detainees and others were moved by train to the interior. Fortunate ones found homes in local communities, but most were housed in makeshift camps with inadequate living conditions and no proper education for interned children. Some families were separated in this relocation process; all lost property. On January 19, 1943, an additional Order-in-Council gave the BC government the right to liquidate all Japanese property that had been left in protective custody.

This lost property was never recovered. In 1988, Prime Minister Brian Mulroney acknowledged the harms done by the actions of the Canadian government through the internment of Japanese Canadians. Compensation packages in the amount of $21,000 for each individual directly wronged were offered.

At the end of the war, Japanese Canadians were forced to start over. However, they were not allowed to return to their homes. The choice they were given was either to return to Japan—a place many had never been—or to relocate east of the Rockies. The level of a significant military threat was never evidenced during or after the war. In 1949, Japanese Canadians received the franchise and were given the right to live where they chose. Very few returned to British Columbia.

Although the story of relocation and internment was a story that unfolded in British Columbia and Alberta, anti-Japanese racism pervaded the country. The Canadian Council of Churches attempted to find homes that would sponsor interned Japanese families, much as they provide sponsorship for international refuges today. The Council found no churches willing to take them up on this invitation. In fact, the Council received only one letter; a congregation in Saskatchewan wrote that if a Japanese family showed up in their community, they would "run them out of town on the rails."

After World War II, the story began to shift in Canada for immigrant groups and their descendants who had arrived from non-English-speaking countries. Slowly, the idea that all persons had basic rights that allowed them free movement and equal access to jobs, spaces, and opportunities began to take hold. The extent to which that basic idea is internalized within the Canadian social fabric is a matter for ongoing debate and reflection. We are left with many questions. The colonizers, themselves newcomers who did not belong, assumed for themselves the right to define the boundaries of belonging and unbelonging in a new land. To enforce that hegemony on the new landscape, Original peoples were moved and other newcomers were invited in regulated form according to their assessed utility to the new social vision. They were then placed on a map geographically and socially to enshrine the myth of White supremacy and European culture dominance. The gridlock, in lockstep with social place, has become unimaginably difficult to deconstruct.

The Black Experience

The subjugation of Black bodies through slavery was one of the most blatant forms of racism to ever take place in the history of our existence, and Canada was no less complicit in slavery as France, Britain or the United States. The first recorded history of Black slaves in Canada was in 1632, although evidence suggests the presence of Black slaves as early as 1607 (Winks, 1971, p. 3). Slavery was officially legalized in Canada between 1689 and 1709,[8] and it continued until official abolishment on August 1, 1833 (Trudel, 1994).

The 1834 official commencement of the abolition of slavery had very little impact on ending anti-Black racism in Canada. The abolition of slavery was followed by more than 100 years of legalized segregation, with the Common School Act of 1850 enshrining segregated schools and classrooms, segregated combat units in armed forces, and segregated public spaces that disallowed for comingling of Blacks and Whites. These policies were eventually recognized as explicitly racist, and de-legislation of racism followed, with the last segregated school closing in 1983.[9]

Just as abolition of slavery had little impact on racism, so too did "desegregation" or the "deracializing" of Canadian policies on halting racism in Canada. In fact, efforts at deracializing served to embed racism as a hidden activity in the fabric of the society, and as a result, racism has become a normal part of everyday life. Although Canada has ideologically deracialized the racial discourse by not explicitly using racist or racial categories, this discourse may—and often does—have a racist effect. During the past several decades, the literature has highlighted this very notion. J. Walker (1985) noted that although "legal reforms have restrained openly hostile behaviour, they have not affected the essential factors leading to discrimination.... The basic issue in Canada has been racial stereotyping" (p. 24).

Nelson (2010) explored the experiences, histories, and cultural engagements of Black Canadians, challenging the myth that Canada is a racially benevolent and tolerant state by foregrounding issues of institutional racism against Blacks in academia and its everyday effects. Traditional institutions of racialized research largely ignore the disparate social and political exposures confronting people of color, such as residential and occupational segregation, racial profiling, tokenism, discrimination, racism, and the consequential physiological and psychological effects flowing from the macro and micro effects of such interactions and intersectionalities. Many race scholars (e.g., Fournier, 2002; T. Smith, 2014; Henry & Tator, 2006) unsettle the origins of Canada's racist history and collusion of various social institutions in the perpetuation of the trope of "Black dangerousness." Police brutality and criminalization of Blackness are vivid examples of the impact such constructions of Blackness continue to have in Canadian society.

Challenges of Diaspora

The notions of diaspora and belonging bring with them issues of identity politics. Belonging becomes tenuous particularly when dealing with migrant and racialized groups, given the peculiarities of their migrant past. For instance, questions of identity and belonging remain problematic for Caribbean people because of their cultural past engagement with slavery. The significance of the search for identity in the lives of Caribbean peoples is closely connected to the immigration experience. As noted by Shelly-Robinson (2004), "This historical factor [slavery] further compounds the search for an identity when as immigrants we find ourselves in countries where we are regarded as second class citizens and so must struggle even harder to find a place of belonging" (p. 3).

Highlighting similar challenges migrant populations face in negotiating identity and sense of belonging, Ahmed (2000) noted that "migration is defined against identity; it is that which already threatens the closures of identity thinking" (p. 82). Much of the diasporic literature brings to the forefront the effects of migration on one's identity and sense of belonging. Negotiating sense of belongingness amid the migratory experience, from all accounts, is an intensely intricate process, and particularly more so for racialized peoples.

One of the significant challenges is how one, both as an individual and as a part of a diasporic group, is come to be known within particular space. The notion of the Caribbean woman as the drug mule is highly gendered but also speaks to the politics of identity for this group. Similarly, the representation of Jamaicans as "aggressive" or Filipino women as nannies speaks to how we belong and where we can belong because our existence within any given space is coded. Hence, it becomes much easier for an Asian woman to find employment as a waitress because that is what "she is good for" as opposed to the job for which she is really qualified.

The weight of such racialized tropes then become the lens through which the marginalized and oppressed person views him- or herself. Racialized identities are internalized, and the process even of imagining a different Self is limited by the inward projection of an outer lens. Part of the struggle with diasporic belonging, then, rests in the intermingling of the experiences individuals and groups bring to the space as well as those that are impacting and being imposed on individuals and groups within that space. A mutually reinforcing prison of narrow vision keeps the whole society, and most notably the marginalized person, bound.

Diaspora brings to the forefront the issue of the stranger in the midst. This discourse of "stranger-ness" accentuates the challenges of belonging to space. The idea of the stranger is highlighted in Ahmed's (2000) work, *Strange Encounters*, in which she deconstructs the notion of "stranger fetishism" and lays bare the fact that many aspects of our society rely heavily on a process through which the stranger becomes an abstracted, universalized figure. Ahmed noted that

> it is the enforcement of the boundaries between those who are already recognized as out of place (even other fellow residents) that allows those boundaries to be established. The "ideal" community has to be worked towards and that labour requires failure as its moment of constitution. (p. 26)

One of the tensions to belonging that is particularly unique to diaspora is the emotional and tangible connection of diasporic groups to their home country. This connection can be shown in diverse ways—cultural, political, and economic. It ranges from expressing the desire to return to sending remittance to family and from participating in cultural and political organizations abroad to engaging in demonstration and petition to impact the home country's political life. This emotional and tangible connection for many people, although regarded as positive toward the home country, can be viewed as a barrier to belonging to the host country. In fact, research shows that for women, finding belonging in diaspora thwarted their attempts to achieve sense of belonging in the larger society (Hogarth, 2011). Diaspora has rules of inclusion and exclusion similar to those in the White space. This was found to be particularly true for Muslim women. A number of these women shared about being excluded and their experiences of not belonging because they decided to not wear hijabs. While in the White space, racialized women sensed they were excluded on the basis that they were not or could never be "Canadians"; in the diaspora, some women believed they were excluded because they were "becoming too Canadian." Adopting more of a Canadian accent, "dressing White," or otherwise relinquishing some of their own culture were signals for exclusion from the diaspora for many women.[10]

Diaspora is about host and homeland as well as the in-between spaces that erupt between the host and the home. In this sense, it is both at the same time geographical and political; it is not only that one occupies space but also how one occupies and comes to be known in that space that determine how the story will unfold. Diaspora interacts with gender and the highly gendered experiences of certain migrant communities. Given the highly gendered construction of care, it inevitably means that women enter and experience diaspora in significantly different ways compared to their male counterparts. They become space spanners and placeholders, their very bodies stretched across the chasm of bicultural alienation in ways that incline toward breaking. Exploring the stress of diaspora in the embodied realities of immigrant women provides a clue to what is necessary for the movement toward a societal stance of non-racism: Space must be created for the "Other" to be both–and/insider–outsider/away and home/here and there/in and out. Women's bodies in every culture span worlds to create the possibility of thriving for the next generation. This is most acutely true in the embodied spaces of racialized women pushed up against the margins of social unbelonging in our culture.

Shifting Notions of Diaspora

Throughout the course of history, shifts in the conceptualization of diaspora have occurred. Although today there is still a great emphasis on race, ethnicity, and geographical informed diaspora, there is at the same time a movement away from the singularity of race, ethnic, religious, or place-based identity. For example, Alvarez (2008) identifies a music-related diaspora of Indigenous reggae artists and their fans based on their "shared struggles for dignity in the face of the dehumanizing effects of globalization." (p. 576) Alvarez is not alone in this conception. Waligórska (2013) asserts that different modes of musical sociability inspire "imagined communities" that not only transcend national borders but also challenge the boundaries between the Self and the Other, suggesting that cosmopolitan understandings of identity might challenge identity hierarchies by moving away from place-based categorizations. Lee and Brotman (2011) introduce the idea of sexual minorities as diaspora communities, and Pecic (2013) intersects the fields of queer and diaspora studies in an investigation of Western notions of sexual identity and belongingness alongside post-colonial deployments of nation, diaspora, and sexuality.

One of the latest shifts is the movement toward the notion of e-diaspora, which takes into consideration how technology is impacting on movement and influencing sense of belonging of people groups in transition. The concept of e-diaspora was formed out of the complex relationships that emerged between diasporic groups and their usage of information and communication technologies (ICTs), especially in the ways these groups use ICTs to achieve community-specific goals.

The term *e-diaspora* emerged at the end of 1990 along with the spread of the Internet and the development of many online public services. During the past decade, there has been a vast increase in web usage as well as social networking media such as Facebook, LinkedIn, and Twitter by migrant populations. In defining e-diaspora, Diminescu (2012) described it as a "migrant collectivity as it organizes itself and acts particularly on the web, and whose practices are those of a community whose interactions are 'enhanced' by digital exchange." There is a significant level of instability because the collective often changes with each newcomer. However, it is a heterogeneous entity whose existence rests on an elaboration of a common direction—a direction not defined once and for all but which is constantly renegotiated throughout the evolution of the collective. Conceivably, e-diasporas are not bound by ethnicity or ethnic origins, geography, or even language, although these may be the unifying threads of some e-diasporas. The World Wide Web networks aid in the development of decentralized communities and provide an ideal avenue to create an imaginary transnational collectivity.

The diffusion of technologies, finances, and cultural migrants has created a new concept of place and community that can no longer be viewed only in local terms. The very notion of globalization is centered on the interconnectedness of social, political, economic, and cultural relations in the world. One effect of this interconnectedness is seen in the movement of capital and labor, and also in immigration from the Global South to the North. Teferra (2004) also suggested that the unparalleled developments in

ICTs have quietly revolutionized the way the skilled human resource operates and circulates.

Advances in technology have also created opportunities for migrants to maintain close, ongoing ties with their homeland in a way that was not possible in the past.[11] Studies in transnationalism show that there is a growing trend among many immigrants to maintain close contact with family, friends, and co-nationals in diaspora while keeping up with events taking place back home, as opposed to becoming completely assimilated into their host country and cutting ties with their homelands. The new ICTs play a key role in the maintenance of these ties. New migrants are free from territorial constraints because it is possible for them to simultaneously be both "here and there" and take actions transnationally. ICTs have created new ways of being and new patterns of transnational action, helping people network across ethnic, regional, and religious divides.

With the rise of ICTs, immigration is neither a one-way movement nor a loss for the home country for immigrants. The diffusion of Internet and ICTs has helped make it possible for migrants to stay connected to their home countries. The impact of globalization has given rise to significantly increased ways in which immigrants can stay actively involved in the economic, cultural, social, and political life of their home countries. Financial remittances, Internet communication and travels, diaspora and hometown associations, and other means through which immigrants can live abroad and stay connected to their country of origin all serve as potentially vital developmental tools.

ICTs play a special role in the construction of what we may call the diasporic public sphere because they allow new forms of agency in the building of imagined communities. In fact, Appadurai (2003) noted that the sense of "nation" can be formed in cyberspace, and often cyberspace serves as the sole means of providing a sense of aspiration and hope to placeless migrant populations, thus making e-diasporas critical for the formation and sustenance of community for immigrant groups.

One of the greatest potentials in the trend toward e-diaspora is in diminishing the sense of "stranger-ness" of the diaspora. The "facelessness" of an e-diasporic community mitigates some of the challenges associated with traditional forms of diaspora. E-diasporas are able to transcend geographical boundaries and because of advances in technology are able to access and participate in the life of both home and host communities in increasing and more substantial ways. E-diasporas provide a way of circumventing some of the political and systemic issues that diasporas are usually afflicted with; unfortunately, however, e-diasporas do not address these issues directly.

Conclusion

While everything changes, everything stays the same. The discourse on diaspora must inevitably engage issues of global deterritorialization, but in the midst of such, there is the global reclaiming of territory that gives greater rise to transnational movements and the formation of diasporic groups. Shifting notions of diaspora offer us a glimpse into borderless, deterritorialized spaces in which diaspora can exist. These spaces nonetheless do not provide a complete escape from the challenges traditional diasporic communities experience. Challenges to belonging and citizenship still remain even within e-diasporic spaces.

The history of diaspora for particular ethnic groups in Canada is deeply interwoven with experiences of racism that inform how diaspora and belonging are negotiated and experienced. There remain several challenges for "Othered" belonging in Canadian space, many of which pivot on the axis of race. Individual experiences of racism are in fact not isolated but, rather, tied to the social and systemic and have a significant impact on how racialized bodies and diasporic peoples experience belonging in strange lands. Advances in technology not only increase access to participate and hence achieve a greater sense of belonging but also serve to blur the lines between the personal and the political. The challenges associated with stranger-ness are also somewhat diminished in the shifting notions of diaspora. In the blurring of the sharp edge of cutting "Otherness" that technology offers, we glimpse the creative space beyond racism/anti-racism to non-racism—the deeply creative space in which Self emerges from an unboundaried territory of relatively neutral space undefined by the hegemonizing will of a self-designated power-holding group.

4

Canadian Multiculturalism

ON THE WORLD STAGE, Canada has long been known by the image of mosaic. In contradistinction to its American melting pot neighbor, Canada chose the image of the mosaic very early in its story to describe how it understood the relationship of difference in its national identity. Writing in 1938, John Murray Gibbon produced a now famous work that laid the foundation for this self-representation: *Canadian Mosaic: The Making of a Northern Nation*. Interestingly, this work was written during a decade of significant restriction on Canadian immigration for most groups globally. The economic challenges of the era meant that Canada worked to stem the inflow of new immigrants. However, *Canadian Mosaic* does not address restriction but, rather, documents the prior decades that had witnessed an influx of waves of immigration from a variety of national beginning places, and it paints a celebratory affirmation of the richness of a national heritage that would be fashioned from the wide cultural differences that immigrants from many nations would bring. Gibbon talked about the need to formulate a national consciousness among newcomers, but he stressed that this was well under way, with "cement" for the Canadian mosaic being provided by several pillars of the emergent social fabric. The churches, the YMCA, Boys Scouts, Girl Guides, various voluntary women's organizations, and the school system all served to teach not only English language but also Canadian culture through the inculcation of values such as hygiene, thrift, and hard work. Gibbon viewed the diversity of this new immigrant nation as its greatest strength.

Building on its mosaic imagery, a social imaginary was fashioned along the heterotopic model of Foucault. In 1971, Canada became the first country in the world to adopt multiculturalism as an official policy. This policy, implemented in the era of Prime Minister Pierre Trudeau and reflecting his vision for Canada, affirmed the value and dignity of all Canadian citizens regardless of their racial or ethnic origins, their language or their religious affiliation. It confirmed the rights of Aboriginal persons and the status of Canada's two official languages—English and French.

The theory of Canadian multiculturalism is fundamental to the nation's belief that all citizens are equal. It ensures that all citizens can keep their identities and can take pride in their ancestry while at the same time have a sense of belonging in the broader sweep of Canadian society. It encourages racial and ethnic harmony and cross-cultural understanding. It contends that a spirit of mutual respect helps develop common attitudes. It assumes that new Canadians no less than other Canadians respect the political and legal process and want to address issues by legal and constitutional means. Through multiculturalism, Canada recognizes the potential of all Canadians, encouraging them to integrate into society and take an active part in its social, cultural, economic, and political affairs. All Canadians are guaranteed equality before the law and equality of opportunity, regardless of their origins. Canada's laws and policies recognize Canada's diversity by race, cultural heritage, ethnicity, religion, ancestry, and place of origin and guarantee to all men and women complete freedom of conscience, thought, belief, opinion, expression, and right to peaceful assembly. All of these rights, as well as freedom and dignity, are guaranteed through Canadian citizenship, the country's Constitution, and the Charter of Rights and Freedoms (as brought into effect in 1982). Currently, the policy of multiculturalism has led to higher rates of naturalization than ever before, with the legalized guarantee of no pressure to assimilate and or to give up one's culture. Immigrants are free to choose citizenship or not. Assuming the same basic shared value of democracy, Canadians of all points of origin are free to choose, without penalty, whether they want to associate with their specific group of origin or not. Their individual rights to choose are protected as a matter of law from group pressure either to assimilate or to resist assimilation.

This is the theory that undergirds the Canadian policy of multiculturalism. For those who prize respect for diversity, it is an admirable and inspirational policy. The challenge, of course, is that the policy and its application are not necessarily the same thing. In the following discussion, we explore the manifold challenges that exist, both historically and currently, to the successful implementation of this policy vision. However, the purpose of the exploration is a movement away from a social imaginary that by way of embedded racism cannot realize its own hope for itself toward an anti-racist perspective that supports the possibility of the practical realization of genuine multiculturalism within Canadian society.

Questions have been raised as to whether the expressed commitment to multiculturalism as a way of expressing statehood is in fact viable at all. If a nation state is in fact a multinational state, is it anything at all? Apart from questions of national identity, however, are the more pressing questions of quality of life. These are insider questions: How shall we live on the inside of a world that purports to value equality and dignity beyond any external categories of difference? Canada has chosen for itself a social imaginary whereby we eschew the racialized hegemony of a dominant class in favor of one that shares power through respect for difference as a matter of law and practice. The intention of this book is to move the discourse forward, understanding that an anti-racist perspective and its reception and application are an indispensable pathway for that conversation.

A necessary endeavor is the problematizing of Whiteness juxtaposed against people of color and how the normalizing of Whiteness impacts conceptualizations of multiculturalism. Our application of the term *multiculturalism* does not simply herald the notion of cultural pluralism, as in a nonheterogeneous society, although it encompasses it. Our use of the term is also reflective of an ideal of a culturally egalitarian society that holds the tension of cultural particularity, on the one hand, and notions of equality, on the other hand. Another aspect of our definitional use of the term is in reference to the policy of official multi-culturalism embraced by Trudeau's government in 1971 and reinforced by the Canadian Multiculturalism Act passed by Canadian parliament in 1988.

Black Canadians

The story of Black communities in Canada has a long history. To enslave another human being is the most extreme form of dehumanization. It reflects the practice of discrimination taken to the outer limits of imagination. Only Black Canadians and First Nations persons had the experience of legalized enslavement in the Canadian story. For both groups, slavery ended with a change of law in the British Empire in the first half of the 19th century. However, slavery for Black Canadians was more common than for native Canadians during the early period of British rule. The enslavement of First Nations persons under colonial powers was more known in the period of New France than it was after 1763, given the imperative of the Royal Proclamation to extend the hand of friendship to Indigenous communities.[1]

The first persons of African descent known to have arrived in the area of North America that is now Canada came in the 1500s. In the period of New

France (1628–1763), Black persons lived as slaves in the region now known as Quebec. During this period, approximately 1,000 persons lived as slaves, working mostly as household servants. After the period of the American Revolution, another 2,000 Black slaves arrived with Anglo United Empire Loyalists who had fought on the side of the British. As well, another 3,500 Black Loyalists arrived as free persons, to receive grants of land promised to them for their service in the Revolutionary War. Most of these Loyalists settled in Nova Scotia. During the War of 1812, when the British fought back American attempts at encroachment, another 2,000 Black persons came to British North America (BNA) to receive land in exchange for their military service.

Within the British Empire, the movement to end both the traffic of slaves and slavery was underway. In 1793, in Upper Canada, the parliament passed the Act to Limit Slavery in Upper Canada. This act represents the first legislation in a British colony to restrict slave trade. While the act recognized that slavery was a legally and socially acceptable institution, it prohibited the sale of new slaves into Upper Canada. Although no one was freed because of the legislation, nor was the sale of slaves prohibited, it did prohibit any further importation of enslaved person into the region from elsewhere.

In the Empire more broadly, legislation was passed by the British parliament to end the slave trade in 1807 and to formally abolish slavery within it in 1833. This meant that BNA would become a potential safe haven for persons enslaved south of the border. The United States did not abolish slavery until 1865. Prior to this, slavery had been abolished in the northern states. However, the Fugitive Slave Act of 1850 meant that slaves who had escaped from the southern states to the north could be recaptured and returned to slave holders. This fueled the energy for escape north of the border into the British colony. It is estimated that between 15,000 and 20,000 African Americans settled in BNA between 1850 and 1860, increasing the Black population by a considerable margin to approximately 60,000 persons. Blacks who entered Canada during this period through the agency of the Underground Railroad a series of routes followed by fugitives, occasionally with the help of free African Americans and white abolitionists in the northern states found new lives in a variety of occupations and professions. Although their access to power was limited by the discriminatory laws of the day, most found ways to carve pathways toward strong contributing lives in Canadian society.

Throughout the first half of the 20th century, Black Canadians suffered from the various forms of marginalization that plagued other minority groups. As was the case for Chinese children in Victoria, British Columbia, there were some instances of school segregation in the province of Ontario.

In the southern area of the province, notably Chatham and Windsor, where historic Black communities were strong, schools were segregated for Black children. The last segregated Black school in Ontario (Merlin) was closed in 1965. Access to certain public spaces was also restricted throughout the country, as was inclusion of Blacks in the military for much of World War I. The message of racialized unbelonging for each group was writ large and unquestioned across a broad swath of the social landscape. People were moveable, dispensable, and disposable according to their racial classification and their economic utility, defined capriciously by the moment in history and the geography in which they found themselves.

One of the most infamous incidents of just such a dispensability in the history of Black Canadians was the debacle at Africville in the 1960s. Africville was effectively a suburb of Halifax, located near the ocean. It was one of the oldest Black communities in Canada, originating as a community built with slave labor in the mid-18th century. In 1947, the City of Halifax made the decision to turn Africville into an industrial area. Citizens of the community resisted this decision. However, throughout the 1950s, the view of Halifax was that Africville had become a slum neighborhood that reflected poorly on Halifax. Despite community resistance, the City of Halifax voted to "reclaim" the neighborhood. Beginning in 1964 and continuing for 5 years, the community was torn down one property at a time, including the bulldozing of the church, a focal point for community action and life in 1967. Through a "home for home" deal, homeowners were supposed to be compensated for their property. However, in most cases, the compensation was insufficient to replace the homes lost.

The overwhelmment of the rights, liberty, and property of the residents of Africville reflected a contemporary version of the community displacement that had happened to First Nations communities in the prior century. The arbitrary use of municipal authority at the expense of the autonomy of an entire community is notable, even in a nation in which the idea of individual rights and freedoms was just gathering momentum.

Antisemitism and the Story of Jewish Canada

Antisemitism as a social othering device has been present in the story of Western culture for millennia. It is distinct from racism narrowly defined as we are using it here because it predates the very idea of race. As noted in Chapter 1, human cultures have always defined what is normative and what is "outside," and they have always discriminated against or scapegoated particular groups. Jews throughout history have often found themselves in this

"Othered" role. Prior to the othering of Jews because of race, the story of Western history shows antisemitism, or discrimination against the Jewish community, rooted first in religious discrimination and second in ethnic discrimination.

Our prior argument is that discrimination because of "race" is an invention of the modern era. Within that generalization, the category of antisemitism is unique. Although a "racial" classification for Jews was firmly in place by the era of National Socialism (description of the physical and genetic characteristics of Jews as a group), they did not fit into the original classification of key "races" that emerged through the Enlightenment—categories that were defined predominantly on the arbitrariness of "color": white, black, red, and yellow.

A Jewish person could be any of these "colors." To formulate a racial argument based on the post-Enlightenment idea that skin color defined race was not possible with reference to persons of Jewish ancestry. As such, other physical attributes were cited, such as head size and shape, as well as nose physiology.[2] However, the physical characteristics named here were not as significant as a lens that had been developed as early as the Middle Ages. Although the idea of race as an identifier in modern terms did not exist, there was by the Middle Ages the idea that Jews were different from other people as a matter of "blood." In medieval Spain, there was the introduction of purity of blood laws relating to religious practice and the initiation rite of baptism. Christians were considered of pure blood. Both Jews and Muslims were not. The physical categorization of blood purity was linked to religious practice. A baptized Christian was of pure blood, and the person was all the more pure if he or she was born into a family of already baptized and practicing Christians.[3]

We see in this the long-standing intertwining of religion in the definitions of "other" and the justification of discrimination in Western society. From the later 4th century, Western culture named Christianity as the "normative" if not proscribed religion. Those who stood outside the practice of Christianity were "Othered" and as a matter of law discriminated against. Across centuries, the force of law was placed behind this categorization of normativity in a variety of ways. The social legitimation of scapegoating Jewish persons first for their religion and later for ethnic and racial reasons was broadly accepted as normative across Western cultures. It was this reality that allowed the Holocaust to be perpetrated by the National Socialists in Germany and beyond, to act against Jewish persons with impunity. The assumption broadly held that Jewish persons were less than human, or at the very least not entitled to the rights of human beings under the law, was a necessary precondition to the Final Solution.

Racialized Antisemitism

Building on the blood notions of medieval antisemitism, National Socialism developed racial theories congruent with Enlightenment categories but specifically adapted to the idea of "eugenics." The emergent theory of eugenics took racial theory to a new level by postulating the notion that a process of genetic selection could eliminate social problems through the genetic purification of the human race. Hitler and his associates divided human beings along racial lines defined through the emergent science of genetics. Germanic peoples were named as "Aryan";[4] all others were non-Aryan. The German people shifted in Nazi ideology from being an ethnic group to being a racial group—a racial group that was superior to all other races. Race-based antisemitism in Germany was enshrined as matter of law through the Nuremberg Race Laws of 1935. These laws covered every area of human life and opened the door for the total loss of life and liberty of the Jewish people, defined as the archetypal inferior race by National Socialism.

Although Canada joined Britain in the battle against Germany in World War II, it was not because of opposition to the racial policies that Hitler and his followers promulgated. Rather, in Canada during the time of the war, one witnessed the continuing segregation and exclusion of Jewish persons in a variety of geographic, social, political, and education settings. As well, Canada joined a league of other nations that refused to welcome Jewish persons who were attempting to escape from the Europe of the Nazi era. In the now famous work *None Is Too Many*, Canadian writers Irving Abella and Harold Toper (2012) documented the story of Canada's relationship to Jews through the period of National Socialism. The title of this book was taken from what is now an infamous quotation by a high-level Canadian immigration official. Speaking in response to a question as to how many Jews Canada would take during the era of their persecution under National Socialism, Frederick Charles Blair, Secretary of the Immigration Branch of the Department of Mines and Resources, stated, "None is too many" (p. 9). During the 12-year period of the Nazi regime, only 5,000 Jewish refugees were allowed to enter Canada, whereas most other allied countries admitted tens of thousands.

Although notably anti-Semitic, Secretary Blair was not singular in his views. The general tenor of the Canadian government in the prewar and war eras was notably anti-Jewish. The government of then Prime Minister

William Lyon Mackenzie King viewed Jewish immigration as a significant threat to Canadian society. Three weeks after Kristallnacht in 1938, Prime Minister Mackenzie King and Secretary Blair issued the following internal office memo about Jewish immigration:

> We do not want to take too many Jews, but in the present circumstance we do not want to say so. We do not want to legitimize the Aryan mythology by introducing any formal distinction for immigration purposes between Jews and non-Jews. The practical distinction, however, has to be made and should be drawn with discretion and sympathy by the competent department, without the need to lay down a formal minute of policy.

In the face of the extremism of National Socialism, the Canadian government did not want to be associated with overt fascism. However, the quiet way in which racist policies were reinforced made it all the more difficult to deal with what was underneath the public face of Canadian life.

For decades, Jewish persons had been viewed by Canadians as "unassimilable." This was due in large measure to the lack of conformity to Christian practice and the particular "ethnic" rituals linked with the Jewish faith. In 1939, Wilfrid Lacroix, Member of Parliament for the province of Quebec, presented a petition to the House of Commons signed by 123,364 individuals from throughout Quebec speaking against Jewish immigration. An editorial piece in *La Presse* (January 31, 1939) following the petition affirmed the rightness of its direction, stating, "The Jew can neither adapt nor assimilate and he will therefore never be a citizen of the country where he lives; he is an inevitable cause of trouble and disturbance" (p. 13).

The most disturbing story of exclusion from this era took place in 1939, when a luxury liner named the St. Louis set sail from Hamburg, Germany, with 907 Jewish refugees aboard. All had visas to land in Cuba. However, when the ship arrived in Cuba, entry was denied. All Latin American countries were approached for permission to land. All denied permission to land. The ship set sail with the hope of finding harbor in either the United States or Canada. Permission in both cases was denied. The ship returned to Germany, and most of the 907 passengers died in the Holocaust (Abella & Troper, 2012, pp. 63–64). This rejection of refugees during this period was mirrored elsewhere in the world, including in the Mediterranean, where one boatload of refugees was sunk off the Turkish coast by a Soviet submarine after its engines failed and it was not allowed to dock in Istanbul to repaid its engines.

A total of 781 refugees and 10 crew members died. Interestingly, during this period, the Chinese opened their doors to more than 20,000 Jewish refugees, who built vibrant communities in Shanghai.

Jewish Immigration

Jewish immigration into Canada was part of the national story from early days. The first Jews known to have settled in Canada arrived in Quebec in 1760 as part of a British military contingent. As early as 1832, the British colonial government recognized the right of Jewish persons in the colony of BNA through the adoption in the legislature of Lower Canada of the Act to Grant Equal Rights and Privileges to Persons of the Jewish Religion, which ensured that Jews in Lower Canada would have basic civil and political rights. Interestingly, Lower Canada was the first jurisdiction in the British Empire to afford these rights as a matter of law to the Jewish community. Even so, the first wave of significant Jewish immigration did not take place until the late 19th century. As a response to increasing violence against Jews in Eastern Europe, a mass migration out of Europe to other areas of the world began to unfold. Between 1871 and 1901, the number of Jewish persons in Canada increased from 1,333 to more than 16,000. As part of the large immigration wave discussed in the preceding chapters, more than 60,000 Jews came to Canada between 1901 and 1911. More than half of that number took up residence in the province of Quebec, the location of the first Jewish immigration.

In 1919, the community of Jewish persons in Canada was significant enough in size that the Canadian Jewish Congress was founded. Its purpose was to serve as a vehicle for unifying and supporting Jewish immigrants as they attempted to make a new life in Canada. As discussed in the preceding chapters, immigration policies were very restrictive during the inter-war years, particularly through the depressions. In 1930, the Canadian parliament enacted legislation that barred all immigration from Europe, except for those with adequate resources to support themselves on farms and those with immediate family already in the country. This was of particular import to the Jewish community because at that time most Jewish immigration was from Europe. In 1931, further legislation limited immigration to American and British citizens of either independent means or who were in the primary industries, such as mining, farming, and logging. Between 1921 and 1931, only 15,800 Jewish immigrants entered Canada. Circa 1931, approximately 156,000 Jews were living in Canada, and the population remained constant at this level until hostilities in Europe had ceased. After World War II, immigration rules eased somewhat for Jewish persons, and through the efforts of the Canadian Jewish Council, between 1946 and 1960, as many as 46,000 Jewish immigrants came to Canada.

The Tenor of Canadian Antisemitism

What did antisemitism in Canada look like? As suggested previously, Canadian antisemitism historically has been both overt and covert, depending on the situation and circumstance. Also as previously discussed, early Jewish immigrants to Canada offered significant contributions to the development of the newly emerging nation. However, both dominant Anglo-Christian society and Francophone Catholic society echoed the strains of antisemitism that was achieving such play on the world stage. Through the 1920s and 1930s, anti-Semitic rhetoric grew in both political and social circles.

The Social Credit Party (SCP) was openly critical of the Jewish community as a racial group. Founded in 1932, the SCP of Alberta was elected as a majority government in 1935 and remained in power until 1943. The SCP found resonance with the Albertan electorate through its strident call to capitalism as a palliative for the economic ills of the Depression. It believed that aggressive capitalism was the only way out of the Depression and that those to blame for the economic disaster of the 1930s were the communists and the Jews. This platform found a ready audience in the Albertan population. Interestingly, at the time, Jews made up less than half of 1% of the Albertan population.

A new organization called the Native Sons of Canada was chartered in 1922, and from its origins in British Columbia, it very quickly became a nationwide organization with more than 100 assemblies or chapters. Its aims were expressly the promotion of Canadian nationalism, but a nationalism that defined the new Canada as Anglo and White. Immigration from "Orientals and Jews" was discouraged. Anti-Semitic rhetoric peppered the organization's documents, faulting the Jewish community as antagonistic to the national vision it promoted. Limitations on the social spaces that Jews could occupy abounded.

In 1933, one year after Hitler's rise to power in Germany, latent anti-Semitic tensions broke out in a massive riot in Toronto's Christie Pits. On August 16 of that year, there was a baseball game at Christie Pits park between a local Catholic boys team, St. Peter's, and Harbord Playground, which was predominantly a Jewish team. St. Peter's was in the lead. Near the end of the game, a group of young men from the neighborhood showed up and unfurled a banner with a Nazi swastika on it. As soon as the boys from Harbord Playground saw it, they left the field and charged the swastika bearers. A riot broke out that lasted more than 6 hours, with hundreds of people, both Catholics and Jews, descending on the park and participating in the violent conflagration using whatever weapons they could find. It is arguably the worst incidence of public violence in Canadian history.[5]

Also in 1933, the Canadian Nationalist Party was formed. This small group of men was composed of ex-military personnel who chose to don the brown shirt of the fascists and promote an anti-Semitic agenda akin to the fascism of continental Europe. This group had a publication titled *The Canadian Nationalist*, through which the messages of German National Socialism were promulgated. In Canada, however, this activity was checked as a matter of legal prohibition in 1935.

This course correction notwithstanding, general anti-Jewish sentiment continued. In 1938, a National Fascism Convention sponsored by the National Unity Party was held at Massey Hall in Toronto. It was not held without resistance, however. The conference had originally been planned to be held in Kingston, but conference organizers in the end declined to rent space to the fascists for this purpose. The conference was thus held in Toronto, but opposition was expressed by the local branch of the Legion and the League for Peace and Democracy. The League held an antifascist rally in opposition at Maple Leaf Gardens that drew a much larger crowd than the conference held by the fascists (Davies, 1992, p. 126).

Beyond the political arena, antisemitism was pervasive and implied. Throughout the pre-war years, quotas were assumed: Only so many Jews were allowed in a wide sweep of venues. There were Jewish lawyers—often discriminated against in courtroom proceedings—but no Jewish judges. Jewish doctors often could not find appointments in hospitals. Many industries expressly would not hire Jews. There were very few Jewish teachers, and quite often other professionals such as engineers, nurses and architects hid their Jewish ancestry as a necessary means of procuring employment. The sale of private property was often "under covenant" so that it could not be sold to Jewish persons. Public spaces such as beaches, resorts, and golf courses were often restricted, disallowing Jewish membership, with signs warning "No Jews or Dogs Allowed" or "Christians Only" as a means of ensuring the message was clear.

After World War II, the horror of the Holocaust forced antisemitism off the stage of Canadian public life for the most part. However, although no longer acceptable in the way it had been prior to the war, antisemitism has continued in Canadian society as an undercurrent that affects public discourse and occasionally has manifest as outbreaks of public violence.

In 1948, noted Canadian author Pierre Burton went undercover to research and write an article on antisemitism in Canada for *Maclean's* magazine. Originally published in November 1948, Berton's article, "No Jews Need Apply," explores the "discrete country-club style antisemitism" that was rife in Canadian society in the post-war years. His research led him to conclude that "people with names like Greenberg" were frequently denied job interviews, promotions, hotel and country club reservations, and the right to live in certain neighborhoods. Berton's observations reflect the challenge of dealing with racism in Canada: It is often difficult to pin down but observable in the experience of those who are on the receiving end of it.

In 2015, the B'Nai Brith Society of Canada released an "antisemitism audit" that indicated that in the preceding year, 2014, there had been an almost 30% increase in anti-Semitic incidents in Canada. For more than 30 years, Canada's senior Jewish human rights agency has monitored the levels of antisemitism in the country. In 2014, there were 1,627 reported incidents of anti-Semitic activity. This observed trend is not unique to Canada but, rather, is reflective of a surge in antisemitism globally.

What, then, can we say about antisemitism in Canada? Antisemitism, as with many other forms of racism, has been mainstream in Canada. Until the era of civil rights, the assumption of an anti-Jewish position was not atypical nor a cause for ostracization. It reflected the social imaginary of much of Canadian society, for much of its history. Antisemitism existed in every region of Canada. It was socially and geographically pervasive. With the implementation of the Canadian Charter of Rights and Freedoms in 1982, the table was re-laid. Statutes and laws have been remade. Jews along with all other members of Canadian society were promised their rightful place at the table of citizenship. As with the other stories we have been exploring in this text, living up to that promise has been the difficult work of making a new world at the level where people actually live.

A History of Arabs in Canada

The first account of Arabs in Canada dates back to 1882 with what can be considered the first wave of Arab migrants.[6] During this first wave of Arab immigration, Canada welcomed fewer than 3,000 Arabs up to the period of World War II. Between 1911 and 1961, Canada imposed restrictions on Asian entry into the country. These restrictions were also applied to Arabs, who were then classified as Asians. The period of restrictions saw limited numbers of new arrivals with fewer than 10,000 Arabs entering Canada during the post-war era up to 1967. Those who were within the borders of the nation became firmly settled and integrated into the society.[7] The lifting of immigration restrictions from 1962, along with factors closely related to wars—such as Al-Nakba in Palestine in 1948, the Suez War of 1956 following the Egyptian Revolution of 1952, the Six-Day War of June 1967, the 1973 War, the civil war in Lebanon, the Iran–Iraq War of 1980–1988, the 1991 Gulf War and subsequent invasion and occupation of Iraq in 2003, the civil wars in Sudan, Somalia, and Algeria, and the continuing Israeli occupation of Palestinian territories—led to a significant rise in Arab immigration to Canada. The distinction is often made between the two waves of Arab immigrants, with the latter being more highly educated and having stronger links to the Arab world. Prior to 1975, the majority of Arabs who entered Canada were Christians and mainly from the Macherk, who lived under Ottoman rule. The third wave of Arab immigrants arrived during the period from 1967 to 1990, when Canada welcomed almost 100,000 Arab immigrants. The recent Syrian refugee crisis further adds to the numbers in the Arab Canadian population. Since 1990, close to 1 million Arabs have entered Canada as immigrants. Since 2009, Canada has permanently resettled nearly 25,000 Iraqi and Syrian refugees. In January 2015, Canada expanded its commitment to resettle an additional 10,000 Syrians; this goal was met in September 2016.[8]

Islamophobia

Islamophobia did not suddenly emerge after the terrorist attacks of 2001. Within Western culture, the story of fear and vilification of Muslims, as well as the violent suppression of Muslim communities, can be found as early as the Middle Ages: The Muslim hordes were to be limited and suppressed. In more contemporary valance, the history of global crisis politicized as Arab wars has significantly influenced the global consciousness of the precariousness of political and social stability. The crisis of September 11, 2001 (9/11) has forever changed relationships between the dominant group and Arabs in Canada, erupting latent fears and introducing new ones. In the 2-month period between September 11 and November 15, 2001, 115 incidents of various forms of hate against Muslims in Canada were documented.[9] The politicization of Islamic identity often translates into the articulation of the Islamic body, perceived or practicing, as an oppositional identity. In this regard, Muslim identity is constructed as a response to terrorism, on the one hand,

and victims, on the other hand. However, the media and political rhetoric that has informed the consciousness of the populace even begins to challenge the possibility of a victim identity for Arabs generally and Muslims specifically.

Islamophobia can be said to constitute various forms of racism, including both epistemic and cultural racism. It is both political and personal, and it is constructed in the blurriness of the boundaries where religion has been distilled down to the cultural. The belief that Islam and Western values are in contradiction helps fuel the antagonism within which Islamophobia thrives.

The government's response to the terror of 9/11 and the ongoing unrest in Arab countries was to further systemically enshrine anti-Muslim racism in the fabric of Canadian society. In October 2001, Canada revealed its new anti-terrorism legislation. This was in keeping with similar laws passed in the United States and Britain in the aftermath of the 9/11 attacks. The four principal objectives of the government's plan were to keep terrorists out of Canada and to protect Canadians from terrorist acts; to procure tools to identify, prosecute, convict, and punish terrorists; to ensure that the Canada–US border remains free and safe for the sake of the Canadian economy; and to coordinate efforts at an international level to prosecute terrorists and deal with the causes of hatred (Department of Justice Canada, 2001).

Subsequent acts were passed supporting the objectives of the 2001 legislation. In 2002, the Canadian Air Transport Security Authority Act was passed. This act allowed for heightened levels of airline security and screening of passengers and baggage. In addition to this act, another response came when the Canadian Security Intelligence Service (CSIS) was given increased abilities to collect information on its citizens suspected of terrorist engagement. In a featured address greeting, the director of CSIS noted that "there are violent people and violent groups that want to kill Canadians. It's a sobering observation to make, and there is no euphemistic way of making it." He went on to make the link between the Islamic State in Iraq and "extremists who return to this country more radicalized than when they departed."[10]

One of the other responses to 9/11 was Bill C-51, the Anti-terrorism Act. This act encompasses airline security, financial transactions and banking, law enforcement, immigration and citizenship, taxation, and surveillance. In 2015, this act received royal assent and became law in Canada. Under this act, persons can be convicted of collateral crimes, such as facilitation,[11] without proof of criminal intent or even knowledge of a terrorist act. The far-reaching effect of this act means that even lawyers representing the legal rights of accused terrorists are placed in the precarious position of potentially facing prosecution for "facilitating" terrorist activities as a result of representing clients.

Canada also adopted during this time a political discourse that promoted Islamophobia, and the media helped in framing the stage for anti-Muslim racism. In 2015, Parliament also passed into law the Zero Tolerance for Barbaric Cultural Practices Act, the focus of which is explicitly on immigrant communities ignoring the very same activities existing in Canada's White communities. The act creates a false dichotomy between "immigrant" honor killings, which to date in Canada there have been 17, and, for example, the hundreds of Indigenous women who have been murdered or have gone missing at the hand of their intimate partners. What is particularly worrisome about this act is its veiled references to Muslims. Well noted by the Bridge Initiative is the policy rhetoric of the act that brings into question its intent and consequences:

> In many ways, this law is similar to the "anti-Sharia" bills that appeared (and, in some cases, passed) in numerous American states. Like the anti-Sharia laws, the "barbaric practices" act offers solutions to problems that don't exist, and focuses unwarranted attention on Muslims while ignoring concerns posed by other groups.[12]

When the new government announced the intake of Syrian refugees, one of the discourses that erupted centered on the Islamization of Canada. The fear among the populace was that with such great influx of Syrians, Canada would be forced into being an Islamic state. There are many misconceptions embedded in this fear, not the least of which is the representation of all Arabs as Muslims. The notion that the values of Islam are antithetical to Canadian values and being a Muslim equates disloyalty to Canada as a nation is highly problematic. Since 9/11, there has been continuous debate on balancing security, freedom of religion, freedom of expression and civil liberties—hijab, niqab, kirpan, yarmaluke, religious holidays, and so on. It is in this rhetoric of safety and security that we construct the terrorist Other and label them Muslim. These constructions of the terrorist, within the framework of the Canadian response, have had significant impacts on Muslims in Canada.

Such was the case of 21 Muslim men of Indian and Pakistani origin who were arrested in Toronto in August 2003 under "Project Thread" for allegedly being part of an al-Qaeda sleeper cell (Walkom, 2003). One of the men spent 44 days in protective custody at a maximum security jail before being released without any criminal or security-related charges being laid. In a similar case, labeled the "Toronto 18," 18 men, including 4 youth, were arrested in the summer of 2006 for allegedly being part of an al-Qaeda type cell. Charges against 7 of the accused were subsequently dismissed. These are by no means isolated cases. In fact, using the law to justify the violation of human rights, particularly of Muslim and Arab Canadians, has become commonplace.

Difference, Belonging, and Multiculturalism

The question we focus on here is how does difference, in the multiplicities of cultures, ethnicities, and religions, come to belong within the Canadian multicultural landscape? If we understand multiculturalism in a very simplistic and pedestrian way, as cultures existing in the same space, then we can see Canada as a multicultural utopia. In this unnuanced and uncritical way of understanding multiculturalism, culture is devoid of values and norms and Whiteness goes unchallenged. In this sense, multiculturalism negates the acceptance of difference as a productive dynamic by viewing it as that which must be overcome or simply accepted.

The intent of Canadian multicultural policy, however, is to move beyond such a simplistic understanding and incorporate notions of acceptance and equality of all cultures. As stated previously, multiculturalism conveys the idea of promotion of tolerance and understanding among different groups and bridges the divide between assimilation and the creation of ghettos where minority groups are ostracized. It was designed with hopes of being the means whereby individuals can freely participate in civil society and engage in the promotion of shared values that underpin our society while accepting the differences that serve to enrich our collective dialogue. Thus, in multiculturalism, everyone is presumed to be equal.

The concept of Canada's multiculturalism policy has two critical emphases: (a) the maintenance of heritage, cultures and identities and (b) the full and equitable participation of all ethnocultural groups in the life of the larger society. The pursuit of either of these ideals in exclusion of the other leads to opposing but equally devastating outcomes. On the one hand, pursuing the maintenance of culture without a pursuit of equitable participation leads to separation at the individual level or segregation at the wider societal level. On the other hand, emphasizing participation without the maintenance of culture leads to assimilation at the individual level or melting pot at the wider societal level. At the very core of the multiculturalism policy is the idea that there would be mutual group acceptance of the notion of maintenance of heritage and cultures. However, theories in ethnocentrism tell us differently. Throughout history, it has been demonstrated that the more groups, communities, and societies positively evaluate their own ways of being, the more they negatively evaluate the ways of being of others. This ideal of a mutual acceptance of the culture of others becomes challenging.

Still, the Canadian multiculturalism policy is based on the premise that only when people are secure in their own identity will they be in a position to accept those who differ from them—that is, when there is no threat to their identity. In his announcement of the policy, Prime Minister Trudeau highlighted this premise. He noted (Statement to House of Commons, 8 October, 1971, Government of Canada, Ottawa)

> National unity if it is to mean anything in the deeply personal sense, must be founded on confidence in one's own individual identity; out of this can grow respect for that of others and a willingness to share ideas, attitudes and assumptions. A vigorous policy of multiculturalism will help create this initial confidence. It can form the basis of a society which is based on fair play for all. (p. 8545)

This premise engages with the Self/Other construct in which the identity of the Self is carved and solidified in how we construct the Other. Although this is a theoretical truism, the equation on which the premise is based is faulty. The premise suggests that out of a construction of Self that is based on the view of the Other, we will arrive at an egalitarian society. However, the history of nations has taught us that one does not lead to the other, and it is more likely, taking into consideration all of the societal constructions around difference, that in the gaze of the Other we arrive at an inflated construction of the Self, which then lends justification to the domination and supremacy over the Other.

Multiculturalism provided the framework through which all groups could hope to belong in Canada. It was framed at a time when Canada faced internal and external threats to its nationhood. Legare (1995) suggested that this was not coincidental. He noted that

> from the start, it was "intended to ground Canadian nationhood in an identity that could be differentiated from threatening Others both within and without." Prime Minister Pierre Trudeau believed that multiculturalism could serve as "the glue of nationalism," a glue that could bind a uniquely defined nation, governed by a strong federal government. As a solution to internal divisions, official recognition of multiculturalism within a bilingual framework could counterbalance the contesting regional loyalties that endangered the unity of the nation.

At the same time, by accepting all ethnically defined claims as equally valid, it could effectively neutralize nationalist claims to special status or rights, re-establishing and strengthening national unity. (p. 350)

In a positive interpretation of both the policy and the practice of multiculturalism, immigrants are seen as easily integrating into mainstream society. From this perspective, the social supports necessary for successful immigrant integration are accounted for in the practice of multiculturalism. In his book, *Strangers at the Gate: The Boat People's First Ten Years in Canada*, Beiser (1999) suggested that immigrants feel welcome in Canada because they do not feel the pressure to shed their cultural identities immediately upon entering Canada. They have time, and the necessary community supports, to help them settle in Canada. These sentiments were also articulated by Weinfeld (2002) in his book, *Like Everyone Else But Different*. He described Canada as "a post-biblical Garden of Eden, for those seeking both participation in the general society and a vibrant Jewish culture" (p. 26).

Needless to say, the ideal of multiculturalism is different from the practice of multiculturalism in Canada. The ideal of multiculturalism provides a context within which we can begin to engage the question of how the Other comes to belong within spaces that are constructed with the veneer of inclusion but with a practice of exclusion based on factors such as race, gender, and culture (defined in relation to a "dominant normative"). The notion of national unity embedded within the framing of multiculturalism gives us a lens through which we can view nationalist sentiments in viewing the Other as a threat to national identity. Within this context, differences in values and religious practices threaten the very stability of the nation state and therefore must be contained. Multiculturalism then becomes an act of containment and control that reifies the outsider status of immigrants, particularly those who are distinctly different by virtue of ethnicity, culture, race, and religion, through a range of patriarchal, racialized, and nationalist cultural discourses that strip away rights and relegate migrants to political, social, and economic marginality.

Canadian multiculturalism still ties us to a relatively static model of culture and moves us away from an analysis of the complexity of inequalities. Redhead (2002) argued that "Trudeau's multiculturalism policy was not so much an attempt at promoting the development of different cultural groups as much as it was, quoting Trudeau, 'basically the conscious support of individual freedom of choice'" (p. 59). In this regard, power differentials were not taken into account, and what multiculturalism has become is a way of both hiding and enshrining power relationships. One of the problems that arise through multiculturalism's focus on culture was taken up by Ahmed (2001). She noted that

> the emphasis of culture over and above issues of political economy or at least the refusal to understand culture as a site of struggle that is also political and economic—means that multiculturalism neutralizes the differences that it apparently celebrates: The social accommodation afforded through cultural pluralism avoided the potential of social disharmony by channeling the social and economic strivings of migrants into the private domains of their cultural needs. (p. 105)

The paradox of Canadian multiculturalism policy is that although it officially encourages cultural difference, it works to extinguish diversity. Not only is the ideal of tolerance and celebration of genuine diversity impossible in such a world but also the notion itself becomes intolerable.

Within the practice of Canadian multiculturalism, we see the reproduction of the colonial code. Despite the celebratory rhetoric of diversity, notions of Canadian multiculturalism are inextricably linked with the development of Canada as a First World society creating new forms of colonial control in the so-called post-colonial era. Multiculturalism remains centrally the consumption of other cultures, where White and the dominant culture never enter the arena. It becomes an act of voyeurism where difference is paraded as the dominant culture indulges its appetite for the exotic until it reaches the point of satiation. In the language of bell hooks (2000), multiculturalism is the consumption of what is desirable about cultures and the vomiting out of what is not, all the while maintaining hegemonic relationships and keeping the status quo in perfect balance.

If, in fact, we are to engage in a critical way with the notion of multiculturalism, we must begin to question the normativity of Whiteness as a formidable challenge to sense of belonging for racialized Others. In the multicultural imagining, Whiteness does not exist as race. The normalizing of Whiteness further entrenches the dichotomies of the "us" and "them" and perpetuates stereotypical presumptions about people of color—Whiteness is not a race: It becomes the Norm. An interrogation of Whiteness is critical to a better understanding of how racism is perpetuated and maintained through state-sponsored initiatives. As noted by Fine (1997),

> Whiteness, like all colors, is being manufactured, in part, through institutional arrangements. This is particularly the case in institutions

designed as if hierarchy, stratification, and scarcity were inevitable.... Whiteness and color are therefore not merely created in parallel, but are fundamentally relational and need to be studied as a system. (p. 58)

Problematizing Whiteness in the context of multiculturalism is in fact one way of forming and policing the racial boundaries of White supremacy and racism.

Although multiculturalism may offer a promise to facilitate belonging, it is not working, and along with transnational practices, it leads to the fragmentation and segregation rather than the integration of diverse racial, ethnic, and religious groups. Daniel Stoffman's (2002) *Who Gets In* raised serious questions about the policy of Canadian multiculturalism. He suggested that multiculturalism works better in theory than in practice. One of the most common criticisms of multiculturalism is that the policy promotes hyphenated-Canadians, fragmentation, and the inability of society to develop a cohesive identity. Neil Bissoondath (1994), in his book *Selling Illusions: The Cult of Multiculturalism*, maintained that Canada's multicultural policy has been "quietly disastrous for the country, and for immigrants." (p. 1) He asserted that Pierre Trudeau's Liberal government assumed that "culture" could be transplanted and that immigrants would wish to bring their culture of origin with them. He described the festivals by different cultures as "folkloric Disneyland." In some sense, the Canadian multicultural policy creates mental ghettos, leading immigrants to feel divided loyalties. Not only are differences highlighted but also individuals are defined by their differences. The result of Canadian multiculturalism is the lack of integration of immigrants into the Canadian mainstream and, subsequently, a weakened sense of Canadian identity. We see then again the racialized body of the immigrant woman stretched across polarities that, in these terms, cannot be covered/reached.

Beyond this weakened sense of identity, Canadian multiculturalism poses several problems for immigrants. As noted by the Multicultural Health Broker Co-operative (2004), Canada's multicultural reality does not embrace "the principles of equality, tolerance and the protection of individual rights, essential ingredients for an open and inclusive society" (p. 6). This is clearly demonstrated through the political rhetoric of safety whereby various acts are passed into law that ultimately target and limit the very freedom and individual rights of particular immigrant groups. In contradiction, it seems that in reality the discourses of multiculturalism and diversity serve as a means of sustaining hegemonic relations between immigrants and the dominant society and its structures and muting the experiences of immigrants. The mechanism of hegemonic relations through the state policies of multiculturalism is evident in Canada's representation as a welcoming haven for immigrants and refugees, whereas in reality these policies work to create structures that keep immigrants, particularly racialized immigrants, in a marginal social, political, cultural, and economic relationship with Canada, even as they work to limit the place and possibility of Indigenous Canadians:

> We know that there is no hope for this current generation. However, if we persist in our efforts among the Indian people perhaps the grandchildren of this generation may be raised up to the level of a servant class in Canadian society.[13]

In a critical assessment of Canadian multiculturalism using a liberal multiculturalist view, we can see the limitations of the policy through its celebration of diversity without confronting oppression. One need not look far to see the various forms of oppression immigrants and particularly racialized immigrants face. Although the stories of the many highly skilled immigrants who are driving taxis in Toronto may be slightly inflated, it remains a fact that immigrants are grossly underemployed and make up the greater percentage of Canadian unemployment. A Statistics Canada (2015) report indicated Blacks, particularly those originating from Africa, had the lowest employment rate in Canada.[14] The marginalizing of immigrants and First Nations peoples through the erection of barriers that effectively keep them out of the workforce falls within the definition of oppression and easily translates to a lack of respect for the difference embodied in the immigrant and the Indigenous. It has been proven repeatedly that one of the reasons for the high unemployment rate among immigrants is the unwillingness of Canadian employers to accept anything that is not "Canadian," including language, accent, education, and color. This has become so much of a barrier to immigrants' meaningful engagement in the workforce that in 2013 the Ontario Human Rights Commission approved a policy on removing the "Canadian experience" barrier to immigrant entry into the labor market.[15]

Central to the multicultural policy is the concept of "tolerance" for "other" cultures. "Tolerance" carries with it an unsettling feeling of not to be liked but merely tolerated. Our multicultural ideal may in fact support a degree of tolerance, but beyond a certain point, on the far edge of equality, it asserts "Canadianness" and warns off "others" from making claims on Canada. The constantly posed question to immigrants of "Where are you from?" is a way of asserting "Canadianness" while indicating that the immigrant is not, and cannot be, "Canadian" but will always be "from somewhere else" and thereby reifying supremacy in space and time. With this in mind, Anthias and Lloyd (2002) suggested that debates on critical multiculturalism must necessarily

> move away from the idea of one dominant culture that lays the frame of reference for the existence of tolerance towards other cultures. As such it must maintain a view of citizenship where the boundaries of citizenship are not coterminous with belonging to a community in the singular. (p. 13)

Despite the intent of the Canadian multiculturalism policy to tolerate diversity, Whiteness still remains an essential feature of "Canadianness" and, as such, difference along color lines remains a barrier to integration.

The very terminologies embedded within multicultural discourses, such as "integration" and "tolerance," have a huge impact in shaping social relationships. These terminologies are not benign; instead, they carry meaning for both the mainstream and the Othered. Inscribed within these terminologies are weights and measures of who holds the responsibility for doing what. The message that is received by immigrants is that it is their responsibility to "integrate" while at the same time it is the mainstream's responsibility to "tolerate" the immigrant and racialized Other.

The ideal of multiculturalism aids in the creation of an imaginary state, but when set against the backdrop of reality, it fails to deliver on the promise of truly belonging. The imaginary of a multicultural ideal is fueled by a construction of Canada as a gold standard by which to measure the rest of the world as well as a refuge to run to. Canadian multiculturalism is sold through media portrayals and embassies throughout the world as something to be greatly desired, holding great promise of security and belonging. These portrayals help in the creation of an imagined citizenship. However, the imagined, when jarred against the reality, heighten unbelonging. It is in their imagined citizenry that racialized immigrants often construct a sense of belonging. In this regard, Canada is distinguished by its falsities based on the imagined. Given the role of the state in creating an imaginary state through its work in embassies throughout the world and its very deliberate market campaigns, falsity becomes a central distinguishing feature of the imagined multicultural state constructed by racialized Others. Certainly, the goal of multiculturalism is not toleration but, rather, awareness, knowledge, understanding, engagement, respect, and equal place—Is it not?

In the final analysis, the ideal of multiculturalism is quite distinct from the reality. Multiculturalism, diversity, and the many other constructed forms of dialoguing on this are all inextricably linked to racism. In reality, multiculturalism is a tool of management of cultures and identities with racial, ethnic and religious discrimination central to the management project. Instead of addressing the epistemic nature of racism in Canada, we engage in one act after another to solidify race relations and maintain the hegemony. Although Canada prides itself on being a multicultural mosaic in which diversity, equality, and harmony are valued, our reality tells a story that is far different from the ideal. It tells a story of inequalities related to race, ethnicity, and culture. It tells a story of oppression, marginalization, and exclusion from full and meaningful participation in Canadian society. Canadian attempts at multiculturalism generally ignore the sexist, racist, and colonial forces that continue to dominate discussions of Canadian identity. Although multiculturalism is dialogic, how to talk, where to talk and who gets to talk remain significant epistemological issues in multicultural discourse. Therefore, what is wrong with Canadian multiculturalism still remains unaddressed because the voices of those whose lives are most impacted by the structural inequalities created in the system are silenced.

Racialized immigrants have very little opportunity to make reasonable claims against systemic racism when the "system" is positioned to act as both oppressor and savior. Making such claims, then, can easily be, and often is, relegated to the individual immigrant being too sensitive or reading more than is warranted into innocent actions, thereby erasing the immigrant reality and embedding racism deeper into the system. A critical approach to multiculturalism will inevitably be anti-racist and dedicated to social justice and structural change. It must move well beyond the superficial notions that if we all get along and celebrate each other's differences, we will get rid of racism, or if we get rid of ignorance, we will get rid of racism. We have a long history of "getting along" while supporting and further erecting structures that promote inequality along race lines. The discourse must be expanded to include an engagement with power. How we get along is dictated by the "ruling class," and unfortunately we cannot legislate "getting along."

The ideal of multiculturalism holds promise. In the path between reality and ideal, Canadian multiculturalism needs to undergo a radical shift to create a "critical multiculturalism." Such a shift would incorporate an analysis of the inequalities of power that both stimulate and ensue from practices of racial, ethnic, or gender discrimination. A critical approach to citizenship will inevitably be anti-racist and dedicated to social justice and structural change.

Our efforts to define a non-racist space, where we can find breath and place for all to draw according to their unique capacities, are aided by the efforts of post-colonial thinker Homi Bhabha. His writing deftly unmakes the imperial assumptions of the colonizer, arguing that any view of the world that constructs itself on a theory of separate and unequal cultures is doomed to fail. Although he does not take the more extreme stance of his colleague Frantz Fanon, who argues that the bifurcated world constructed by the various impositions of colonial overseers can only be unmade through the violent overthrow of the oppressed by the oppressor, nonetheless he postulates the end of the colonizer's dominance. This end comes through the setting aside of the assumptions of the imperial mind. The colonial world is divided against itself through both a romantic and a naive utopia—weaving a myth of imaginary peoples and places. Both the colonized and the colonizer are not what they are mythically created to be or to mean. In the world beyond the chains of colonization, there is a social space that is composed of diverse social spaces, distinct but not separate (interrelated) and equal. Building on the work of Edward Said, Bhabha talks about the emergence of new cultural forms from multiculturalism. In other words, multiculturalism is a way station on the way to the non-racist space—the Third Space theorized by Soja. In the post-multicultural Third Space is a world in which hybridization becomes the new form of social interaction, as our histories and cultures continue to intrude on our present not as stumbling blocks but as an imperative that pushes us toward transformation of our old forms and outmoded ways of living as communities locked in narratives of subject and "Other." The idea of multiculturalism theorized as the Canadian social imaginary, and yet so historically misconstrued and applied, can only become a possibility through the release of its implicitly hegemonizing underlay- freed to live its discourse about itself, beyond itself.

5

Moving Toward Belonging

IF WE ARE to believe that Canada is a just country in which all its citizens have the same human rights and equal rights to belong, how then do we reconcile the pervasiveness of such experiences as described in Box 5.1 and their links to particular groups outside of the dominant? How then do we reconcile the injustices that have played out for centuries and continue to be enacted in public and private spaces of today's Canada? The hybridity of justice in Canada often means embracing what is just for some and justifiable for others. The binaries of belonging and unbelonging, the Self and the Other, are part of the everyday challenges of racialized and immigrant peoples. The questions Do I belong and how do I belong? and Who am I and who am I to become in light of the dominant Other? form part of the lived experiences of those who are constructed as the Other. As discussed previously, a multitude of factors conspire to create these dichotomies and evoke these questions. Throughout the previous chapters, we engaged with issues of race, colonization, diaspora, and multiculturalism as critical to our understanding of Othered belonging in Canada. We unearthed several challenges within these discourses that would make the task of belonging challenging, if not impossible, for those who embody the markers of difference. To end the story here, however, would be only to tell half-truths. To suggest that the history of racialized Others in the Canadian landscape is only a narrative of how they have been oppressed and acted upon is to do an injustice and does not represent the wholeness of their experience. There is a parallel narrative to be told—one of resistance and space making, one that tells of making strides and triumphing in the face of adversity.

Human beings are incredibly resilient. Despite the best efforts of social systems and discriminatory structures to define and thereby limit the development and participation of some in the broader community, newcomers to Canada from its earliest days have found ways not only to survive but also to thrive. In

> **BOX 5.1**
>
> ### The Case of Brian Sinclair
>
> Brian Sinclair was a 45-year-old double amputee, homeless Indigenous man. In October 2007, he lost both his legs to frostbite when he was found frozen to the steps of a church in the dead of winter. Reportedly, he had approached the church for shelter but was denied. In September 2008, a doctor at a local clinic referred Sinclair to a hospital after Sinclair reported being unable to urinate in the past 24 hours. He wheeled himself to the triage desk in a Winnipeg hospital and spoke to an aide before wheeling himself into the waiting room. He was discovered dead, sitting in his wheelchair, 34 hours after he arrived. Hospital staff assumed Sinclair was drunk or homeless rather than a person in need of medical care. He died from a preventable bladder infection caused by a blocked catheter.
>
> Through an inquest following his death, it was revealed that Sinclair was never asked if he was waiting for medical care and that nurses at the Health Sciences Centre did not help him even as he vomited on himself. By the time he was discovered dead, rigor mortis had set in.
>
> His death was ruled a "preventable tragedy" but not a homicide.
>
> How is it that routines came to be organized such that Indigenous people are met with this kind of systemic neglect? The experience of poverty and neglect, the experience that Brian Sinclair lived through, is not an individual experience.

each of the groups we have considered in this work, examples abound of adaptation that has led to the development of new ways of belonging in the middle of ostracization, particular racial and ethnic groups have developed their own norms and found ways for their cultural groups to thrive and prosper within their own cultural groups and society more broadly. These social ecosystems, self-contained as they were, protected marginalized groups and through that isolation provided space for development of modes of being that would eventually work with changing norms in the broader culture to allow the integration of distinct communities into society without the limitations and barriers previously imposed. The implementation of the multicultural ideal in 1971 reflected the beginning of this. The adoption of Canadian Charter of Rights and Freedoms in 1982 confirmed this direction as a matter of legal entitlement. The project that is ongoing in Canadian society is the working toward the realization of the ideal in all avenues of the culture, as the legal right to full inclusion becomes actual inclusion through the transformation of the social imaginary that determines what life will be for Canadians.

Of course, as we have seen, in many ways the ideal of multiculturalism itself is grounded in the perpetuation of difference that posits tolerance in relation to a hegemonic norm. The idea of distinct cultures, Othered in relation to a norm, means just that. However, what we observe in the Canadian case is that groups excluded from mainstream power and pushed to the margins of society because of their difference found ways to thrive on those margins and, through their thriving, to reinforce the power of their particularity as a vehicle for re-making dominant social discourse when legislation shifted even as limits on the social imaginary were pushed open. This is what the historical narrative shows us: Within the exclusionary parameters or their social, political, and legal marginalization, oppressed groups developed micro ecosystems for survival and flourishing that perpetuated their norms and gave them space to hone their skills at adaptation for survival in the larger culture. Even as they were at best "tolerated," still they became.

A second layer of paradox is present here when one considers Canadian immigration policy. As discussed previously, for much of Canada's history, immigration policies projected a vision for Canada that limited the "non-White" population. When waves of immigration were allowed in the early 20th century, the agenda was overtly assimilationist. For example, as discussed in Chapter 4, William Lyon Mckenzie King's primary objection to Jewish immigration was that he viewed Jews as "non-assimilable." When the Canadian government admitted newcomers, it was with the idea that in partnership with the churches, women's organizations, and education, they would teach new immigrants how to "be Canadian," which meant assimilating to Anglo, Protestant, Euro descent norms. Thus, while celebrating the mosaic of difference as Canada's self-image, it simultaneously worked actively both to marginalize the newcomers and to assimilate them. Despite the theoretical rejection of the "melting pot" of its American neighbor, Canada has framed its "tolerance" as sitting "Other" on the outside of in. This marginalization in the end proved more powerful as immigrant groups developed their autonomous self-replicating microcultures as a means of survival in their new world. This made possible the mosaic principle, which national founders had advocated despite racial and ethnic marginalization. Ironically, however, the principle lives inside microcultures and often microcultures in relation to each other, rather than in society broadly defined.

As the illustrations presented in this chapter demonstrate, the thread that appears to run through all of the racialized communities discussed here, in relation to the flourishing of their communities, is education. In each case, the commitment to education in a variety of forms serving the function both of resistance and of accommodation became the vehicle by which marginalized minority immigrant groups found a pathway to the future. Conversely, education has continued to be the primary obstacle in the renovation of First Nations communities, as discussed later. The importance of education as a vehicle for community lift is significant given that education was also used by dominant interests as a primary tool of hegemonization.

Historian H. Richard Neibhur (2004) developed a theory of "social lift," whereby he argued that communities lift themselves in social hierarchies through a variety of means, including education and selective religious affiliation. His theory was that marginalized or oppressed groups adapted to the circumstances of their oppression by both accommodating and resisting them at the same time. This paradoxical practice develops the skills for reading and surviving within a culture while simultaneously equipping the learner with sufficient "insider" knowledge to undermine or shift the discourse of the system.

Education is an excellent illustration of this phenomenon. As was argued so clearly by Michel Foucault (1988), education, like religion, is a hegemonic force within the superstructure of every society. Its purpose, by definition, is to equip members of a given society to function according to the norms of, and in keeping with, the values of society. Nonconformity with those values and norms is viewed as aberrant and is punished and excluded through things such as the prison system or mental health designations. The key in societal transformation is holding the assimilation and the resistance practices in a delicate enough balance that one can effect social change without being literally forcibly removed from social discourse.

It is argued here that a focus on education in most of the groups of people discussed in this book, along with at least one other significant factor, enabled both the adaptation and the particularization of the racialized groups. The education factor is constant. The second dominant factor is unique in its level of importance to the group under discussion, and we explore these as illustrative in the following sections.

First Nations Communities: An Exception That Proves the Rule

Despite assimilation measures designed to eradicate First Nations language and culture, Indigenous communities survived. Not all languages survived, but many did. Today, there are 53 Aboriginal languages surviving in contemporary

Canada. Although conditions on many reserves remain desperately poor, the movement for Aboriginal self-government has inspired a generation of leaders to rise up and summon their people to forge a new path as distinct and self-governing peoples. The Truth and Reconciliation Commission (TRC), which convened over several years to hear testimony from the survivors of residential schools, produced a report with 94 calls to action that not only addressed a remedy for past harms but also provided proactive plans for building strong Original communities and nations. The TRC remains an active site of resistance and holding the Canadian government and the population at large accountable for the atrocities of residential schools. In so doing, it continues to raise awareness of ongoing issues impacting the well-being of Indigenous communities.

However, a limitation of the capacity of First Nations communities to move forward persists. As noted in the discussion of residential schools, in a case distinct from other marginalized groups, education with Indigenous persons was used for assimilation in a way that was distinct from how education was used in relation to other groups. The children of all immigrants were theoretically partially assimilated through public education from the early 20th century. However, First Nations children were also forcibly removed from their families and educated in a residential model designed to isolate them from any "counternarrative" influences. A counternarrative is one that unmakes the assumptions of dominant culture. Dominant culture is generally predisposed to resist counternarratives, and in the case of First Nations communities, it did this to a level not in play for the other racialized groups through removal from kinship networks.

The legacy of the residential schools was a level of harm that continues to plague Indigenous communities today. The most significant issue that hinders First Nations from moving forward and thriving is the question of appropriate models of education for their children. Although residential schools no longer exist, education of First Nation children in city school boards has produced poor results in terms of high school completion and post-secondary entrance. On reserve, although access to direct Original language and culture education and modeling is more accessible, underfunding and other complex social issues mean that education success is also compromised. Division both between Indigenous communities and between the Canadian federal government and Indigenous peoples also contributes to the difficulty of formulating a clear plan for First Nations education.

Racism and government practices have had a significant impact on Original peoples' resistance to policies. The resistance efforts of First Nations communities related to residential schools culminated in 2008 with Prime Minister Stephen Harper issuing an apology to the Aboriginal community recognizing the years of work by survivors, communities, and Aboriginal organizations to get to this point (Box 5.2).

BOX 5.2

Prime Minister Stephen Harper's Statement of Apology[a]

Mr. Speaker, I stand before you today to offer an apology to former students of Indian residential schools. The treatment of children in Indian residential schools is a sad chapter in our history. In the 1870s, the federal government, partly in order to meet its obligation to educate aboriginal children, began to play a role in the development and administration of these schools. Two primary objectives of the residential schools system were to remove and isolate children from the influence of their homes, families, traditions, and cultures and to assimilate them into the dominant culture. These objectives were based on the assumption aboriginal cultures and spiritual beliefs were inferior and unequal. Indeed, some sought, as it was infamously said, "to kill the Indian in the child."

Today, we recognize that this policy of assimilation was wrong, has caused great harm, and has no place in our country. Most schools were operated as "joint ventures" with Anglican, Catholic, Presbyterian, or United churches. The government of Canada built an educational system in which very young children were often forcibly removed from their homes, often taken far from their communities. Many were inadequately fed, clothed, and housed. All were deprived of the care and nurturing of their parents, grandparents, and communities. First Nations, Inuit, and Métis languages and cultural practices were prohibited in these schools. Tragically, some of these children died while attending residential schools, and others never returned home.

The government now recognizes that the consequences of the Indian residential schools policy were profoundly negative and that this policy has had a lasting and damaging impact on aboriginal culture, heritage, and language. While some former students have spoken positively about their experiences at residential schools, these stories are far overshadowed by tragic accounts of the emotional, physical, and sexual abuse and neglect of helpless children, and their separation from powerless families and communities.

The legacy of Indian residential schools has contributed to social problems that continue to exist in many communities today. It has taken extraordinary courage for the thousands of survivors that have come forward to speak publicly about the abuse they suffered. It is a testament to their resilience as individuals and to the strength of their cultures.

The government recognizes that the absence of an apology has been an impediment to healing and reconciliation. Therefore, on behalf of the government of Canada and all Canadians, I stand before you, in this chamber so central to our life as a country, to apologize to aboriginal peoples for Canada's role in the Indian residential schools system. To the approximately 80,000 living former students, and all family members and communities, the government of Canada now recognizes that it was wrong to forcibly remove children from their homes and we apologize for having done this. We now recognize that it was wrong to separate children from rich and vibrant cultures and traditions, that it created a void in many lives and communities, and we apologize for having done this. We now recognize that, in separating children from their families, we undermined the ability of many to adequately parent their own children and sowed the seeds for generations to follow, and we apologize for having done this. We now recognize that, far too often, these institutions gave rise to abuse or neglect and were inadequately controlled, and we apologize for failing to protect you. Not only did you suffer these abuses as children, but as you became parents, you were powerless to protect your own children from suffering the same experience, and for this we are sorry. The burden of this experience has been on your shoulders for far too long. The burden is properly ours as a government, and as a country.

There is no place in Canada for the attitudes that inspired the Indian residential schools system to ever again prevail. You have been working on recovering from this experience for a long time and in a very real sense, we are now joining you on this journey. The government of Canada sincerely apologizes and asks the forgiveness of the aboriginal peoples of this country for failing them so profoundly.

We are sorry.

a. Excerpted from the text of Prime Minister Stephen Harper's statement of apology as released by the Prime Minister's Office.

One of the more recent acts of resistance among First Nations peoples is Idle No More, founded in 2012 by four women—three First Nations women and one non-Native ally. The impetus for Idle No More events lies in centuries-old resistance as Indigenous nations and their lands have suffered the impacts of exploration, invasion, and colonization. The final straw, as it were, was a reaction to the introduction of Bill C-45, an omnibus bill implementing numerous measures that weaken environmental protection laws.[1] Idle No More seeks to assert Indigenous inherent rights to sovereignty and reinstitute traditional laws and Nation to Nation treaties by protecting the lands and waters from corporate destruction. It calls together the Indigenous communities and their allies to fight for the protection of their treaty rights and their fundamental right to live peaceably on their lands. This protest has sparked many others and, if nothing else, has resulted in more people asking critical questions of the system.

Black Communities

Despite beginning their story, within the Canadian context, in the most desperately of oppressed circumstances, Black Canadians persisted. Limitations on access to education and physical spaces were lifted sooner than with other minority groups. The strength of the Black community and the emphasis placed on education empowered generations of leadership that found place in all pathways of Canadian life.

The factors that appear to have been dominant in the Black experience of adaptation and resistance toward social life are education and the strength in community affiliation or networks. These principles can be seen in the example of the Black community in Toronto. The segregation of Black students within several southern Ontario cities was discussed previously. Segregation was never the norm in Toronto, either at the elementary school level or at the university level. Black children attended class with all others. Black doctors graduated from the city's medical schools. Within the community, there was a strong commitment to education as a necessary vehicle for social thriving. This may in part be reflective of the fact that by the late 19th century there was an affluent population of African Canadians who had immigrated to the area over a long period of time.

The strength of the community and its central role in nurturing social belonging was reflected in part through attachment to the church. The Black Church served as a focal point for gathering the Black community, and over time this expanding immigrant group created necessary supportive infrastructure to nurture a new generation of Black Canadians, notably through education, and new immigrants who came in the next era predominantly from the United States. Part of this infrastructure eased the newcomer transition as Blacks easily found work in the Toronto economy. With economic possibility and education for children, the transition of the next generation to upward social and economic mobility was in most cases ensured.

A History of Black Resistance

One of the greatest resistance efforts of Blacks related to changing their identity as possessions or property to being viewed as people, worthy of possessing rights and dignity. The abolishment of slavery did not happen in a vacuum. Slave uprisings in every country in which slaves existed, including Canada, played a pivotal role in the abolishment of slavery. It was these acts of resistance that gave rise to questioning the value of slavery and helped usher in its abolishment.

The most recent chapter of the Anti-Slavery Society of Canada was founded in 1915. One of the strengths of the Anti-Slavery Society of Canada was its strategic networking in bringing together leading abolitionists, both Black and White, from churches including the Congregationalist and Free Presbyterian, as well as from the business, professional, and political elite.

Many Black slaves were involved in their own redemption as well as the dismantling of the state machinery. Notable among them was Henry Bibb, a rebellious slave who escaped to Detroit in approximately 1840 and began speaking publicly against slavery and organizing abolitionist groups. A decade later, he moved to Windsor and founded the *Voice of the Fugitive,* which reported on the Underground Railroad and colonization schemes. The first issue of Bibb's *Voice of the Fugitive* was published on January 1, 1851.

However, although slavery was abolished, segregation continued in Canada. Movie theaters, schools, churches, and even burial grounds were all segregated spaces where Blacks were only allowed to occupy specifically designated spaces. The case of Viola Desmond tells a story of resistance and space claiming that would eventually lead to changing the Canadian landscape regarding segregation (Box 5.3).

Segregation in Canada was dealt a severe blow as a result of the Viola Desmond case, but more work was necessary throughout the country to break the strongholds of enshrined racist laws and practices that maintained racist structures. By the 1960s, the US Black Power movement provided even greater impetus for Blacks in Canada to organize and unite around issues of

BOX 5.3

The Case of Viola Desmond: An Act of Resistance[a]

In 1946, Viola Desmond was arrested at the Roseland Theatre in New Glasgow. Viola had gone to the Roseland Theatre that evening to see her favorite show. In New Glasgow, a law forbade Blacks from sitting in the downstairs section; it was reserved for Whites only. The White moviegoers wanted her to go upstairs because it was the balcony where Blacks could sit. They called it "A Nigger's Heaven." For her refusal to sit in the Black section, Viola was arrested and charged for violation of the provincial Theaters, Cinematographs and Amusements Act. The 1915 act contained no explicit provisions relating to racial segregation. In fact, throughout Viola's entire trial there was never a mention of the fact that she was Black, and there was a complete absence of any overt discussion of racial issues. By sitting in the Whites only section, Viola owed the city an additional $.01 in taxes, for which she was convicted and fined the minimum fee of $20 with costs of $6 payable to the prosecuting informant. The total amount of $26 was due forthwith in default of which the accused was ordered to spend 1 month in jail. The day of her conviction, Viola Desmond paid the full fine, secured her release and returned to her home. She was deeply affronted by her treatment at the hands of the New Glasgow officials. She was also well known throughout the Black community in Nova Scotia and consequently in a good position to do something about it. She began on a journey of retelling her experience, which was profiled on the front pages of *The Clarion*. This led to the Nova Scotia Association for the Advancement of Coloured People championing Viola's efforts.

On April 15, 2010, almost 65 years after the incident, Viola was given a posthumous pardon—the first ever granted—by the government of Nova Scotia. It acknowledged that the charges brought against Viola, and her arrest, were unjust.

a. The case of Viola Desmond was adapted from Blackhouse (1994).

continued racism and to influence the political consciousness of the Canadian population.

The resurgence of the Ku Klux Klan in the 1970s and 1980s was another challenge to anti-racist efforts in Canada. With no direct action taken by the government, responsibility for eliminating the Klan fell to local community and church groups. In 1980, the Riverdale Action Committee Against Racism (RACAR) was founded with the express purpose of driving out the Klan in Toronto. Opposition groups such as RACAR, collectives from a variety of ethnic backgrounds united in the fight against racism, eventually led to the fragmentation of the Canadian Ku Klux Klan.

The Black Action Defence Committee (BADC), led by Dudley Laws and Charlie Roach among others, emerged as a strong activist voice and a voice of defiance against police brutality in the 1980s. After a string of police shootings of Black men in Toronto as well as a judicial system that continued to promote violence against Blacks through the acquittal of officers involved in these violent assaults, a group of concerned Black activists mobilized to create the BADC. The work of the BADC was the catalyst for change in police oversight in Ontario, resulting in the establishment of the Special Investigations Unit, a civilian law enforcement agency with the power and authority to investigate and charge police officers with criminal offenses. Today, resistance efforts are still ongoing in Black communities in Canada. Issues such as carding,[2] which is specifically targeted against the Black community, remain as part of the ongoing legacy of Canada's racist landscape. In response, groups such as the Network for the Elimination of Police Violence and Black Lives Matter continue to engage as counterresistance.

Jewish Communities

The story of Jewish communities in Canada reflects the resilience we are discussing in a notable way. Despite the ongoing trauma of antisemitism from early days to the present, the story of Jewish life demonstrates consistent adaptation partnered with resistance to marginalization (defined here as retention of core religious and ethnic identity) through engagement with dominant culture, as a vehicle for succeeding in the Canadian context. The two factors most notable in this story are education and commitment to engagement with the dominant culture.

These principles are illustrated in the story of Jewish persons in the province of Quebec. Despite exclusions and limitations, Jewish Canadians—through education, investment, private enterprise, and political engagement—became power holders in many sectors of Canadian society from the first half of the 19th century. In other words, even as legalized racism flourished, so did local Jewish communities.

In 19th-century Quebec society, although small in number, Jews were instrumental in helping build the nascent Quebec economy. For example, the first chartered bank in Canada, the Bank of Montreal, was founded by members of the Jewish community in 1817. The founding of the Board of Trade in 1822 was also the product of Jewish efforts, as was the founding of the first telegraph company in 1847. Many large businesses that became synonymous with Canadian enterprise were founded by members of the Jewish community, including Seagram's. Much of the cultural life that developed in pre-Canada Montreal was also begun in the bosom of Jewish communities, including the Montreal Symphony and the Montreal Museum of Fine Arts.

In 1807, the first Jewish person, Ezekiel Hart, was elected to the Legislative Assembly of Lower Canada. Hart was the first Jewish person to be elected to political office anywhere in the British Empire. In 1832, the legislature of Lower Canada enacted the Act to Grant Equal Rights and Privileges to Persons of the Jewish Religion. In other words, Quebec became the first location in the Empire to grant equal rights to Jews. Throughout the 19th century, the Jewish community, enfranchised and protected by society at large, was able to develop and support many social welfare institutions, including hospitals and other health care facilities, which supported not only Jewish persons but also Quebecois society more broadly.

When Canada became a nation and the legislative context of the broader country was taken into account, the limitations on Jewish persons were much more apparent. However, early beginnings in the province of Quebec are fascinating illustrations of the point we are making here: Despite racialization, communities can thrive and ultimately through social engagement break down barriers between worlds. Education as a centerpiece and determination to engage with "dominant" society were the pivots of that reality.

The movement toward a more inclusive society, in keeping with the Canadian multicultural ideal, was significantly aided by Jewish resistance. The separation of church and state as it related particularly to Christian prayer in schools occurred as a result of such resistance to "all common schools having opening and closing exercises consisting of the Lord's Prayer and reading from the Scriptures" (The School Promoters Education and Social Class in Mid-Nineteenth Century Upper Canada Prentice, University of Toronto Press 2004, p. 128.). The Jewish voice was the loudest in protest of what was deemed religious domination and indoctrinations. Eventually, in 1989 and 1990, Jewish resistance paid off with the overruling of two previously failed verdicts in the Ontario Court of Appeal.[3]

The legal successes in Ontario influenced similar legal decisions in British Columbia (*Russow and Lambert v. Attorney General of British Columbia*,

1989) and in Manitoba (*Manitoba Association for Rights and Liberties Inc. et al. v. Government of Manitoba et al.*, 1992) (Shamai, 1997).

Chinese Communities

Chinese immigrants from the early 20th century, despite the extreme challenges discussed in prior chapters, consistently thrived. Many early immigrants became small business owners because their access to employment by others was limited. Small businesses grew and expanded. In recent decades, immigration from China has dramatically expanded the size of the Chinese community in Canada and its accompanying wealth base. The two key factors in the flourishing of Chinese communities are education and entrepreneurship.

This early tone has become evident in the contemporary Chinese Canadian community. Once bans on immigration were lifted, the flow of Chinese immigrants increased substantively. However, this flow of immigration had a particular character. Given the rise of communism in China, immigration from the mainland was banned, and between 1949 and 1974 only immigrants from Hong Kong, a still capitalist British Protectorate, could enter. The flow of immigration from Hong Kong increased as 1997 approached—the years when Hong Kong was returned to China. In the 1990s, a new form of immigrant restriction came into play: Immigrants could enter, but only if they had adequate financial resource to "contribute" to the Canadian economy. Between 1986 and 2000, Chinese immigrants represented one-third of all business immigrants arriving in Canada. This meant that Chinese Canadian communities that had been characterized by entrepreneurship from their earliest days through small local businesses carried on and expanded that tradition of business contribution to the Canadian economy through engagement in the corporate sector.

The level of Chinese ownership in Canadian real estate and their share in the Canadian economy are well documented. Particularly on the west coast, Chinese investment in real estate has had a huge impact on housing prices and, in turn, on the local economy (Sun, 2015). Chinese immigrants have moved from being the most restricted to the most influential of all immigrants in the Canadian context. In fact, China was the country of birth for the largest single group of immigrants throughout the 1990s. All of this reflects a rather historic relationship between Canada and China: a business arrangement. However, in the post legalized racism era, the power correlation is inverse.

One of the remarkable ways the Canadian Chinese community continues to forge spaces of belonging is through the creation of Chinatowns. Chinatowns stand in stark contrast to notions of assimilation that are pervasive in policy discourses about immigrants. In the early landing of Chinese in Canada, Chinatowns began emerging. These areas were and are regarded as safe spaces for the Chinese community to live, get ready access to food and cultural artifacts, and engage each other socially. Although at first the emergence of Chinatowns was a means of excluding Chinese from full participation in the dominant society,[4] that image has been reclaimed and Chinatowns have been turned into places that are positively enriching for the Chinese population. In every major Canadian city, a Chinatown exists. Chinatowns in many senses serve as witnesses to the resiliency and strength of the Chinese community—that in the face of multiple experiences of oppression, they were still able to thrive.

Japanese Communities

Despite the loss of almost everything during World War II and the relatively slow immigration from Japan in the decades after the war, the Canadian Japanese community has distinguished itself with its commitment to education and social well-being among its members at the local level. The quiet success of Japanese communities is reflected in the key factors of education and persistence.

Even in the middle of the traumas that World War II brought to Japanese Canadians, quiet persistence reigned. Japanese families had always prized education, and even in the conditions of war and internment with no access to regular education, parents worked to ensure that education for their children continued. The level of education among Japanese Canadians has been consistently high. Circa 2001, studies indicated that Japanese Canadians are twice as likely to have a university education compared to the average Canadian.[5] Japanese Canadians, along with other historic immigrant racialized minority groups, now also rank disproportionately close to the top of the economic participation scale (Porter, 2015).

After World War II, Japanese Canadians quietly relocated to new regions and started over. They worked for many years to address the unnamed harms that had been wreaked on their communities. They worked quietly and tirelessly toward a remedy for the trauma of internment, loss of property, and liberty. After many years of persistence, this largely unnamed harm in Canadian history was spoken. In 1988, the Canadian federal government issued a formal apology and reparations in the token amount of $300 million that was allocated to internment camp survivors, a Japanese Community Fund, and the creation of the Canadian Race Relations Foundation. It was not until May 7, 2012, that the legislature of the province of British Columbia, the province where most of the initiative for the internment direction was launched, finally issued a formal apology.

Arab and Muslim Communities

The War on Terror has profoundly shaped Muslim identity in Canada. As noted in Chapter 4, being a Muslim means much more than passively being a victim, although even the very right to claim victim status by Muslims has been challenged given the association of the Muslim identity with that of terrorist. Muslim communities are continuously resistant and challenge the discourses used to scrutinize, marginalize, and demonize them. In a recent book, Verjee (2015) uses the Mississauga's annual Muslim festival—a showcase of the city's diverse Muslim population—to illustrate Muslims' contestation of Islamophobic narratives. She writes,

> The performance of Muslims at the festival uses Celebration Square (a public space or commons) in a subversive way to create a dissenting narrative and takes a central role to counter the Western discourses such as that of securitized identities and niqab issues. (p. 183)

Muslim and Arab resistance must necessarily encompass the freeze-frames in which they have been located through Western eyes. These discourses often frame Muslims as a monolithic that is most often violent, patriarchal, and backward—all of which are in contention with Canadian identity. Consider Disney's representation of the Arab in the well-known and highly acclaimed *Aladdin*. This film, which has earned millions of dollars and has been viewed by a large number of adults and children in the Western world, begins with an introductory song titled "Arabian Nights," which in Disney's original version described Arabian lands as a place "where they cut off your ear if they don't like your face. It's barbaric, but hey it's home." After much controversy and protest by Arabs, the song changed to "where it's flat and immense and the heat is intense. It's barbaric but hey it's home." Throughout the film, the "evil," "stupid," "poor," "violent," and grotesque are portrayed as Arabs, and "good" people are portrayed as Westerners and accentless. The Arab stereotypes in *Aladdin* abound and include the portrayal of women as objects without wills, to be controlled or rescued by the masculine other.

Muslim resistance is also one that is necessarily gendered. Media portrayals often reduce Muslim women to a headscarf—submissive and under the thumb of their violent husbands. Such portrayals are in themselves perpetuating an oppressive discourse that needs to be resisted. For many women, the hijab, a symbol in Western eyes of religious subordination, is in fact a powerful tool of resistance. It is a statement about their identity, something they are proud of and want to proclaim. The hijab for some women, within a culture of "consumption," commodification, and commercialization of the Other, stands as an act of resistance against these very notions. It is through these acts of resistance that Muslims are creating spaces in which to belong.

Expressions of Racism in a New Key

Legalized racism ended in Canada. Racism in its most current form is expressed in systemic and personal forms. Systemic racism as a concept made familiar by sociologist Joe Feagin (2000) in his work, *Racist America: Roots, Current Realities, and Future.* Using historical evidence and demographic statistics, Feagin made the argument that even though legalized racism have been set aside, racism per se persists in systems by which society orders itself. Systemic racism functions such that there is an unequal distribution of resources related to racialized communities and that institutions are overlapping in their commitment to perpetuate modes of being that entrench the marginalization of some over others. Systemic racism intersects with other kinds of discrimination, such as sexism, to perpetuate broadly based discrimination, which is difficult to define and even more difficult to name, address, and redress.

Personal racism, as its name suggests, is in many ways immeasurable. It lives inside the persons who then act out their prejudices against their neighbors, often unconsciously but always creating and perpetuating harm. The transition from the personal to the epistemic is not always evident or acknowledged. In fact, one of the challenges of addressing racism is in the failure to recognize the links between individual/personal acts and institutional and systemic acts. As we attempt to move into Soja's (1996) "Thirdspace," a place beyond racism and anti-racism with some conception of a non-racist society, imagining for ourselves a world in which overlapping and intersecting discriminations are no longer or at the very least named and addressed, it is in the land of systemic and personal racism that we must wander, with eyes open and minds committed to difficult analysis. As difficult as a task appears—this deconstruction of the unconscious and assumed—the illustration of the racialized communities noted previously as they have lived through overt racism and toward communal thriving inspire the imagination with possibility. If education and other virtues can equip the sojourners with the necessary material for deconstructing a past and fashioning a future, then there is hope.

Also central to our endeavor of creating spaces of belonging is how we unsettle the boundaries between the Self and the Other that enable us to reflect on the political effects of this distinction. Lila Abu-Lughod (1991) introduced the concept of "halfies," describing them as people whose national or cultural identity is mixed by virtue of migration, overseas education, or parentage. She argued that culture operates in anthropological discourse to enforce separations that inevitably carry a sense of hierarchy. This argument is significant for its implication that discussions of belonging may be characterized by discourses of inclusion/exclusion that may stem from this hierarchy. This is a core feature of many of the non-Westernized feminist perspectives that hones in on the ability of people to simultaneously inhabit multiple, overlapping, and intersecting spaces.[6] The complexity of the racialized Others' experiences means most fundamentally that their interests and priorities are cut across by race, gender, ethnicity, sexual identity, social class, religion, and so on. Gender cannot be isolated from race or any other of these factors that are so intricately woven into the make-up and function of the racialized Other. However, in attempting to understand these dynamics, it is important not to conflate any of these identities. Each of these statuses is imbued with significant levels of oppression. At the same time, however, borrowing from Ramirez's (2007) discussion on belonging from a Indigenous feminist approach, these statuses are nonhierarchically linked as categories of analysis in order to understand the breadth of oppression racialized Others face as well as the full potential of their liberation in the hope that one day, they can belong full members of this nation state. However, the compounding oppression of these marginalized statuses is what makes the task of negotiating belonging even more challenging. What seems necessary, then, is a movement beyond the dichotomous or binary articulations of identity and belonging toward articulations of multiplicity in identity: both/and worlds. Although there is no clear-cut path to take toward achieving a sense of belonging and integration, there are multiple starting points within discourse, policy, and practice. What is somewhat clear is that attaining a true sense of well-being for the racialized Other can only occur through a paradigmatic shift that transcends binary ways of thinking.

One of the limitations of the discourse on immigrants and racialized Others is its tendency to freeze the racialized Other in time, space, and history. As we build on the resistance effort of the various racialized groups, it is necessary that, if we are to make progress as a nation in this regard, we engage in a process of discursive thawing whereby we no longer rely on the stereotypes and outdated and constructed histories of people to frame the Other. Much of the challenge of inviting the Other into space is linked to how we locate the Other. For example, in our imagining that is informed by media portrayals and misrecorded historical accounts, the Arab Other is constructed as "barbaric" and savage. This is a familiar narrative that also forms part of the history making of our Indigenous peoples in Canada. It is the narrative we sold ourselves in order to justify our dominance and colonization of the Other. If we are to be allies in this process of reconstructing and reimaging an egalitarian society, we must first come to terms with the mythological nature of the narratives we have bought into. We must acknowledge that we have misrecognized the Other and that this misrecognition is gendered, classed, and raced.

Hedican (2013) investigated how racism and government practices have affected Aboriginal resistance to policies through an examination of protest and dissent. In most cases, for both Aboriginal and Others, what we have witnessed is the functionality of the law and its capacity to legitimate the illegitimate (i.e., racism). Poorly enforced or ineffective policies continue to present challenges to the rights and freedoms of racialized Others in Canada. The colonial machinery is still at work. Society is still fundamentally based on the phenomenon of gender and racist differentiation of human beings. Through various policies and actions, we may have made some changes, mostly cosmetic in nature but enough to lull ourselves into believing that racism and colonialism no longer exist in Canada. Knowledge of the historical complicity and duplicity between law and racism constitutes a precondition for understanding the material reality of racism today and our attempts at addressing it.

Given the complexities of race, religion, gender, culture, and the societal constrictions as a result of these frames of difference, those who embody the identity of the Other must necessarily create spaces within which to belong. Within the current political and social landscape of Canada, there is no totality of belonging for the racialized immigrant Other, nor for the racialized displaced Indigenous Other. One of the ways we can make sense of belonging is by situating the racialized and immigrant Other as a microcosm within the context of their families, their diasporic communities, and the White society. In this construction, there is fluidity of movement yet an understanding that

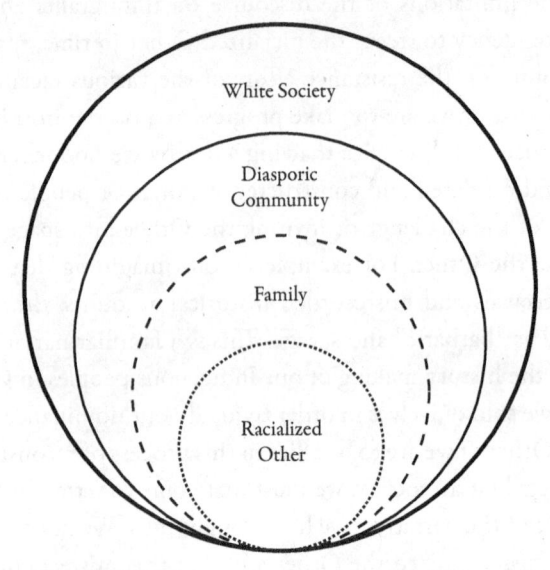

FIGURE 5.1 Spaces of belonging.

we may never achieve true belonging in every space but that there is the opportunity to belong in some space. There exists a greater capacity to move between the spaces closer in proximity to the self. Reciprocal relationships with a level of porosity between the boundaries of these spaces are greatest between individual, family, and diasporic community. Diasporic communities often reflect as spaces in which the raced, gendered, and cultural Other can find a place to meaningfully engage. Although diasporic communities present their own challenges, they also represent microcosmic spaces in which belonging can be achieved. The ease of movement within the White society is curtailed, and movement between the diasporic community and the White society becomes more challenging. Figure 5.1 displays the contextual relationships of these spaces of belonging.

Achieving a sense of belonging within the colonial state that purports an ideal notion of multiculturalism is a challenging undertaking. In each of the cases discussed previously, it can be seen that in fact resistance has not proven to be futile. In every instance, resistance has led to new ways of being and reimagining our reality.

Notes

INTRODUCTION

1. This discussion was first published in Hogarth (2011).

CHAPTER 1

1. An expansion of the classical quotation by existentialist Simone de Beauvoir: "One is not born a woman, one becomes one."
2. Winks (1971) notes that slavery was given its legal foundation in New France between 1689 and 1709 and that had the timing been different, the institution might well have taken a firmer hold than it did.
3. Segregation impacted on every facet of life in Canada and informed who one could marry, where one could go to school, and even where one could be buried. From official records, the last segregated school was in Nova Scotia. See http://www.blackhistorycanada.ca/events.php?themeid=21&id=9.
4. According to Frank Graves, 2015, recent polling shows opposition to immigration has nearly doubled since 2005 and is nearing the 53% level recorded in 1993. Not only is opposition to immigration in general scaling heights not seen in 20 years but also the number of Canadians stating that Canada admits too many visible minorities has recently passed 40% for the first time ever. See https://ipolitics.ca/2015/03/12/the-ekos-poll-are-canadians-getting-more-racist.
5. A Statistics Canada (2013a) report showed that an increased share of recent immigrants to Canada were Muslims. The report noted that in 2011, just over 1 million individuals identified themselves as Muslim on the National Household Survey. They represented 3.2% of the nation's total population, up from 2.0% recorded in the 2001 census. See http://www12.statcan.gc.ca/nhs-enm/2011/as-sa/99-010-x/99-010-x2011001-eng.cfm.
6. Kashmeri (1991) details the experiences of Canadians of Muslim and Arab descent. Also, more detailed descriptions of anti-Arab discrimination can be found in the works of Kutty (2001), Helly (2004) and Franjie (2012).
7. The works of Kinsman, Steedman, and Buse (2000), Henry and Tator (2009), Mascarenhas (2012) and Small (2013) provide some analysis relative to this idea.

8. There is much support for this notion of situating race and racism within a colonial context. See, for example, the works of Vickers (2002) and Wallis, Galabuzi, and Sunseri (2010).
9. There is a general agreement among anti-racist theorists that an interrogation of Whiteness is critical to a better understanding of racism (Dei, 2000; Fine, 1997; Frankenburg, 1993; hooks, 2000; Hurtado, 1999).

CHAPTER 2

1. Mosby (2013) elaborates the specifics of the argument referred to herein.
2. Text of the act circa 1857; see http://caid.ca/GraCivAct1857.pdf.
3. For a comprehensive discussion of reserve and Aboriginal lands in Canada, see Bartlett (1990).
4. For an extensive discussion of the Davin Report, see Truth and Reconciliation Commission (2015).
5. For the full text of the 1948 Declaration and its articles, see http://www.un.org/en/universal-declaration-human-rights.
6. A C. D. Howe Institute study conducted in 2014 showed that the First Nations high school dropout rate has declined, but less so on reserves.
7. Letter from Hoey to Colonel Randle, November 6, 1939; RG 10, Volume 8606, file 487/1-13-001.
8. *Brantford Expositor*, February 27, 1946, and also letter from Gauthier to IAB, DIA, July 25, 1950; RG 10, Volume 6202, file 466-10, part 6.
9. *Brantford Expositor*, February 22, 1946.
10. Letter from Zimmerman to Davey, August 1, 1955; RG 10, Volume 6200, file 466-1, part 4.
11. One of the teachers who worked at the MI in 1930, Susan Hardie, was the product of one such liaison. Her mother had been a student at the MI who was sent to work as domestic help in the home of a prominent Brantford legal mind, Judge Hardie. She returned to the MI and gave birth to Susan. Given that Susan had a "White" father, the DIA would not pay the cost of her support. Her biological father paid the cost of her maintenance at the MI. She eventually went to Normal School and returned to the MI to teach. By 1930, she had taught at the MI for 42 years. RG 10, Volume 6200, file 466-1, part 2.
12. Wolfe (2006) noted that for Indians, non-Indian ancestry compromised their indigeneity, producing "half-breeds," a regime that persists in the form of blood quantum regulations. The restrictive nature of the classification of Indians was necessary because Indigenous people obstructed settlers' access to land and, as a result, their increase was counterproductive.
13. The Truth and Reconciliation Commission (TRC) was established in 2008 as an independent body to provide an opportunity for those affected by the Indian residential schools legacy to share their experiences. Based on those shared experiences

as well as the experiences shared prior to the TRC's existence, a history of abuse emerged. The TRC noted that the unresolved trauma suffered by former students has been passed on from generation to generation.
14. The TRC noted that the policy behind the government-funded, church-run schools attempted to "kill the Indian in the child." See http://www.trc.ca/websites/trcinstitution/index.php?p=39.
15. Blackstock (2003) estimated that there may be as many as three times more Aboriginal children in the care of child welfare authorities now than were placed in residential schools at the height of those operations in the 1940s.
16. Sinclair (2007) noted that "sadly, the involvement of the child welfare system is no less prolific in the current era.... The Sixties Scoop has merely evolved into the Millennium Scoop." (p. 67)
17. Blackstock and Trocme (2005) noted that much of the literature on resiliency is individually focused as opposed to exploring wider cultural, community, and family factors and therefore not lending to a good understanding of the reasons for the disproportionate removal of Aboriginal children from their families.
18. Alfred (2009) noted that there is a high correlation between government laws and policies applied to Indigenous peoples and the negative outcomes experienced in these communities.
19. The 2013 United Nations General Assembly World Happiness Report ranked Canada fifth among world nations. The ranking was based on six factors: real gross domestic product per capita, healthy life expectancy, having someone to count on, perceived freedom to make life choices, freedom from corruption, and generosity.
20. A 2013 study released by the Canadian Centre for Policy Alternatives and Save the Children Canada found that the poverty rate of status First Nations children living on reserves was triple that of non-Indigenous children.
21. See http://www.cbc.ca/news/canada/half-of-first-nations-children-live-in-poverty-1.1324232.
22. Ogunade (2011), through an in-depth economic analysis, showed that where there is an increase in human capital development, there is a corresponding increase in economic development. The reverse is also true. Hence, transferring the human capital from developing countries to the developed world serves the purpose of bolstering the economic development of already developed countries while actively participating in the demise of less developed source countries.
23. Canada was the first country in the world to develop a selection system based on points. Applicants could be awarded 20 points out of a possible 100 for their education and another 10 for vocational preparation. With a pass mark of 50, 15 points (or 30% of the total needed to pass) could be allocated for personal suitability.
24. In the 2002 selection system, education is weighted at 25 and knowledge of English or French at 24. Personal suitability was removed from the selection system.
25. Stark (2002) and others have argued that brain drain may lead to positive results. Even in the poorest of countries, the prospect of being able to emigrate may

increase incentives to acquire education and skills and induce additional investment in education.

26. See Beine, Docquier and Rapoport (2008) and McKenzie and Gibson (2010).
27. The literature is replete with competing terminologies; examples include poor–rich, backward–advanced, underdeveloped–developed, undeveloped–developed, North–South, latecomers–pioneers, Third World–First World, and developing–industrialized. For the purpose of this illustration, any terminology is as good as any other.
28. Goldberg (1993) described the term *new racism* as referring to racial discrimination that involves a shift away from racial exclusionary practices based on biology to those based on culture.
29. Kripalani, Bussey-Jones, Katz, and Genao (2006) noted that "cultural competence programs have proliferated in US medical schools in response to increasing national diversity, as well as mandates from accrediting bodies." (p. 1116)
30. Johnson, Lenartowicz, and Apud (2006) have asserted that the lack of cultural competency in business has led to many international business failures.
31. See the Canadian Nursing Association position statement on promoting cultural competence in nursing at https://www.cna-aiic.ca/~/media/cna/page-content/pdf-en/ps114_cultural_competence_2010_e.pdf?la=en.
32. Acemoglu and Johnson (2007) supported the argument that as a result of colonial intervention, health conditions have remarkably improved, leading to greater life expectancy and hence economic growth of once colonized countries.
33. Alfred (2009) noted that the psychological, physical, and financial dependency created by colonialism and impacting Aboriginal communities is often ignored in the public discourse but that the "cumulative and ongoing effects of this crisis of dependency form the living context of most First Nations existences today" (p. 42).

CHAPTER 3

1. The work of Glenda Simms (1993) on "racism as a barrier" provides a good discussion of this issue.
2. Previous works by the first author speak to the notion of the contested belonging for racialized immigrant women in Canada (Hogarth, 2011, 2015).
3. Instructions to Officers Taking the Dominion Census, Introduction to the Census Report of Canada for 1901, *Fourth Census of Canada 1901*, Vol. 1 (Ottawa, Ontario, Canada: S. E. Dawson, 1902), sections 47–54, pp. xviii–xix, as quoted in *Coal Mines Regulation Act and Amendment Act, 1903* (1904), 10 B.C.R. 408 (B.C.S.C.), at 427.
4. See http://www.macdonaldlaurier.ca/mli-library/books/canadian-century.
5. "The Orientals," in *Methodist Missionary Journal* (1919, p. 132).
6. See http://ccs.library.ubc.ca/en/chronology/chViewItem/1/0/11.

7. It is arguable that the forced migration of First Nations persons is more momentous given the number of persons and the geography that were involved. What is depicted here is the single largest containment and short-term forced movement of peoples on Canadian soil.
8. Winks (1971) noted that slavery was given its legal foundation in New France between 1689 and 1709, and had the timing been different, the institution might well have taken a firmer hold than it did.
9. Segregation impacted on every facet of life in Canada and informed who one could marry, where one could go to school, and even where one could be buried. From official records, the last segregated school was in Nova Scotia. See http://www.blackhistorycanada.ca/events.php?themeid=21&id=9.
10. These were the findings of a larger study conducted by the first author with racialized immigrant women in Canada, exploring their experiences of negotiating belonging in Canada.
11. There is a general acceptance among scholars on the impact of information, communication and transportation technologies on the lives of migrant peoples. See, for example, Cohen (1997), Kivisto (2003), Portes (1999), M. P. Smith and Guarnizo (2002), and R. C. Smith (2002).

CHAPTER 4

1. Note that First Nations groups enslaved each other as a regular practice of conquest and war. The reference here is to enslavement of First Nations people by colonial powers.
2. For a detailed explanation of the physical attributions to Jews by anti-Semites in the modern era, see Hoedl (1997).
3. Note that there was some differentiation and discrimination against converts or new Christian in the Spanish context. See http://matrix.onregional.ca/Matrix/Public/Portal.aspx?ID=0-45341323-10#1s
4. The term Aryan was originated from the self-identification of ancient Indo-Iranian speaking peoples but was adopted by the Nazis to refer to Germanic peoples. The term became synonymous with the idea of a "master race."
5. *Canadian Jewish Chronicle*, August 25, 1933.
6. Karam (1935) recounted the story of Ibrahim Abounadere as being the first Arab migrant to enter Canada.
7. See http://cjms.fims.uwo.ca/issues/10-01/Asal.pdf.
8. Citizenship and Immigration Canada (http://www.cic.gc.ca/english/pdf/syria-infographic.pdf?_ga=1.120850510.732359544.1455200837).
9. The National Anti-Racist Council of Canada indicates that incidents of hate were also reported by non-Muslims presumably mistaken for Muslims, including Sikhs,

Hindus and Arab Christians. See also the National Council of Canadian Muslims website (https://www.nccm.ca).
10. This speech formed part of a featured article by the director of CSIS, Michel Coulombe, in 2014. See https://www.csis-scrs.gc.ca/index-en.php.
11. Section 83.19 provides that "everyone who knowingly facilitates a terrorist activity is guilty of an indictable offence," regardless of whether the "facilitator knows that a particular terrorist activity is facilitated."
12. See http://bridge.georgetown.edu/canadas-barbaric-practices-law-mirrors-american-campaigns-to-ban-sharia.
13. Bishop of the Anglican Diocese of Huron, in a letter to DIA Director written in opposition to the government's decision to close residential schools in 1969.
14. The study further showed that in 2011, these immigrants had the lowest employment rate and highest unemployment rate compared with immigrants born in other regions. See http://www.statcan.gc.ca/pub/71-606-x/2012006/part-partie1-eng.htm.
15. The need for the policy existed in recognition of the significance of all the barriers newcomers potentially face when trying to access the job market. It notes that the policy will focus on "Canadian experience" as an employment or accreditation requirement, and as a practice that raises human rights concerns. See the entire policy at http://www.ohrc.on.ca/en/policy-removing-%E2%80%9Ccanadian-experience%E2%80%9D-barrier.

CHAPTER 5

1. Bill C-45, also known as the Jobs and Growth Act, 2012, covers a number of diverse and unrelated topics changing the legislation found in 64 acts or regulations. The changes that most concern the Idle No More movement are those to the Indian Act, the Navigation Protection Act (former the Navigable Waters Protection Act), and the Environmental Assessment Act. In addition to the changes, those involved in the movement were angered by what they call a lack of consultation with Indigenous peoples. See http://www.cbc.ca/news/canada/9-questions-about-idle-no-more-1.1301843.
2. Carding is the street harassment practice by police officers throughout Canada that involves the stopping and questioning of civilians in noncriminal interactions and documenting their personal information.
3. *Zylberberg et al. and the Director of Education of Sudbury Board of Education* (1988) and *Corporation of the Canadian Civil Liberties Association et al. and the Minister of Education et al.* (1990).
4. In Vancouver, restrictive covenants prevented the Chinese from buying property outside the Chinatown area until the 1930s. For more information, see http://www.thecanadianencyclopedia.ca/en/article/chinese-canadians. Vancouver's Chinatown is currently the largest one in Canada.
5. See http://www.statcan.gc.ca/pub/89-621-x/89-621-x2007013-eng.htm#8.

6. Native feminist, Third World feminist, and Arab and Arab American feminist perspectives find commonality in this notion. The work of Abdulhadi et al. (2011) describes these intersectionalities from Arab and Arab American feminist perspectives. Abdulhadi, R., Alsultany, E., and Naber, N. (2011). *Arab & Arab American feminisms: Gender, Violence and Belonging.* Syracuse University Press.

References

Aboriginal Healing Foundation. (2005). *Reclaiming connections: Understanding residential school trauma amon Aboriginal people: A resource manual.* Ottawa: Anishinabe Printing.

Abu-Lughod, L. (1991). Writing against culture. In H. L. Moore & T. Sanders (Eds.), *Anthropology in theory: Issues in epistemology* (pp. 466–479). Malden, MA: Blackwell.

Acemoglu, D., & Johnson, S. (2007). Disease development: The effect of life expectancy on economic growth. *Journal of Political Economy, 115*(6), 925–985.

Ahmed, S. (2001). *Strange encounters: Embodied others in post-coloniality.* London, UK: Routledge.

Alfred, G. T. (2009). Colonialism and state dependency. *Journal de Sante Autochtone, 2*(2), 42–60.

Alvarez, L. (2008). Reggae Rhythms in Dignity's Diaspora: Globalization, Indigenous Identity, and the Circulation of Cultural Struggle. *Popular Music and Society, 31*(5), 575–597.

Anand, S. S. (1998). Expressions of racial hatred and racism in Canada: An historical perspective. *Canadian Bar Review, 77*(1–2), 181–197.

Anthias, F., & Lloyd, C. (2002). Introduction: Fighting racisms, defining the territory. In F. Anthias & C. Lloyd (Eds.), *Rethinking anti-racisms: From theory to practice* (pp. 1–21). London, UK: Routledge.

Appadurai, A. (2003). Archive and aspiration. In J. Brouwer & A. Mulder (Eds.), *Information is alive* (pp. 14–25). Rotterdam, the Netherlands: V2 Publishing/NAI.

Abella, I., & Troper, H. (2012). *None is too many: Canada and the Jews of Europe 1933–1948.* Toronto, Ontario, Canada: University of Toronto Press.

Austin, D. (2007). All roads led to Montreal: Black power, the Caribbean, and the Black radical tradition in Canada. *Journal of African American History, 92*(4), 516–539.

Backhouse, C. (1999). *Colour-coded: A legal history of racism in Canada, 1900–1950.* Toronto, Ontario, Canada: University of Toronto Press.

Bannerji, H. (Ed.). (2000). *The dark side of the nation: Essays on multiculturalism, nationalism and gender.* Toronto, Ontario, Canada: Canadian Scholars' Press.

Bartlett, R. H. (1990). *Indian reserves and Aboriginal lands in Canada: A study in law and history*. Saskatoon, Saskatchewan, Canada: University of Saskatchewan Press Native Law Centre.

Bauman, Z. (2001). *Community: Seeking safety in an insecure world*. Malden, MA: Blackwell.

Beine, M., Docquier, F., & Rapoport H. (2008). Brain drain and human capital formation in developing countries: Winners and losers. *Economic Journal, 118*, 631–652.

Beiser, M. (1999). *Strangers at the gate: The boat people's first ten years in Canada*. Toronto, Ontario, Canada: University of Toronto Press.

Berton, P. (1948, November). No Jews need apply. *Macleans*.

Bill No. 60: Charter affirming the values of State secularism and religious neutrality and of equality between women and men, and providing a framework for accommodation requests. (2013). Retrieved from http://www.assnat.qc.ca/en/travaux-parlementaires/projets-loi/projet-loi-60-40-1.html

Bissoondath, N. (1994). *Selling illusions: The cult of multiculturalism in Canada*. Toronto, Ontario, Canada: Penguin.

Blackhouse, C. (1994). Racial segregation in Canadian legal history: Viola Desmond's challenge, Nova Scotia, 1946. *Dalhousie Law Journal, 17*(2), 299–362.

Blackstock, C. (2003). First Nations child and family services: Restoring peace and harmony in First Nations communities. In K. Kufeldt & B. McKenzie (Eds.), *Child welfare: Connecting research policy and practice* (pp. 331–343). Waterloo, Ontario, Canada: Wilfrid Laurier University Press.

Blackstock, C., & Trocmé, N. (2005). Community-based child welfare for Aboriginal children: Supporting resilience through structural change. In M. Ungar (Ed.), *Handbook for working with children and youth: Pathways to resilience across cultures and contexts* (pp. 105–120). Thousand Oaks, CA: Sage.

B'Nai Brith Society of Canada. (2015, June 11). B'nai Brith audit reveals anti-Semitism in Canada reaches an all time high. *Edmonton Jewish News*.

Bodvarsson, O., & Van den Berg, H. (2009). *The economics of immigration: Theory and policy*. New York, NY: Springer.

Bryce, P. (1922). *The story of a national crime being and appeal for justice to the Indians of Canada*. Ottawa, Ontario, Canada: James Hope.

Calliste, A. (1991). Canada's immigration policy and domestics from the Caribbean: The second domestic scheme. In J. Vorst et al. (Eds.), *Race, class, gender: Bonds and barriers* (pp. 136–168). Toronto, Ontario, Canada: Garamond.

Calliste, A. (1996). Antiracism organizing and resistance in nursing: African Canadian women. *Canadian Review of Sociology and Anthropology, 33*(3), 361–369.

Chakrabarti, S. (2012). Moving beyond Edward Said: Homi Bhabha and the problem of postcolonial representation. *International Studies: Interdisciplinary Political and Cultural Journal, 14*(1), 5–21. doi:10.2478/v10223-012-0051-3

Chan, W., & Chunn, D. E. (2014). *Racialization, crime and criminal justice in Canada*. Toronto, Ontario, Canada: University of Toronto Press.

Clark, C. (2015, November 25). Trudeau says refugee plan had to change after Paris attack. *The Globe and Mail.* https://www.theglobeandmail.com/news/politics/paris-attacks-changed-refugee-plan-trudeau-says/article27477121

Cohen, R. (1997). *Global diasporas: An introduction.* Seattle, WA: University of Washington Press.

Cuvier, G. (1789). *Tableau elementaire de l'histoire naturelle des animaux.* Paris, France: Baudouin.

Daschuk, J. (2013). *Clearing the plains: Disease, politics of starvation, and the loss of Aboriginal life.* Regina, Saskatchewan, Canada: University of Regina Press.

Davies, A. (1992). *Anti-Semitism in Canada: History and interpretation.* Waterloo, Ontario, Canada: Wilfrid Laurier Press.

Dei, G. S. (2000). *Removing the margins: The challenges and possibilities of inclusive schooling.* Toronto, Ontario, Canada: Canadian Scholars' Press.

Dei, G. S. (2007a). *Keynote address at the symposium on "Multiculturalism With(out) Guarantees: The Integrative Anti-Racism Alternative."* University of British Columbia, Vancouver, British Columbia, Canada, April 2, 2007.

Dei, G. S. (2007b). The denial of difference: Reframing anti-racist praxis. In T. Das Gupta, C. James, R. C. A. Maaks, G. E. Galabuzi, & C. Andersen (Eds.), *Race and racialization: Essential readings* (pp. 188–201). Toronto, Ontario, Canada: Canadian Scholars' Press.

Dench, J. (2007). *A hundred years of immigration to Canada, 1900–1999: A chronology focusing on refugees and discrimination.* Canadian Council for Refugees. Retrieved from http://ccrweb.ca/en/hundred-years-immigration-canada-1900-1999

Department of Justice Canada. (2001, October 15). *Government of Canada introduces anti-terrorism act.* Retrieved January 16, 2016, from http://www.justice.gc.ca/eng/cj-jp/ns-sn/act-loi.html

DiAngelo, R. (2011). White fragility. *International Journal of Critical Pedagogy, 3*(3), 54–70.

Diminescu, D. (2012). *The e-Diasporas Atlas.* Fondation de la Maison des Sciences de l'Homme. Retrieved from http://www.e-diasporas.fr

Feagin, J. R. (2000). *Racist America: Roots, current realities, and future reparations.* New York, NY: Routledge.

Fine, M. (1997). Witnessing Whiteness. In M. Fine, L. Weis, C. Powell, & L. Wong (Eds.), *Off White: Readings on race, power, and society* (pp. 57–65). New York, NY: Routledge.

Foucault, M. (1984). Of other spaces: Utopias and heterotopias. *Architecture, Mouvement, Continuité, 5,* 46–49. (Original work published 1967.)

Foucault, M. (1988). *Madness and civilization: A history of civilization in the age of reason.* New York, NY: Knopf Doubleday.

Franjie, L. (2012). The "clash of perceptions" in Canada since 9/11: A study of the Canadian Arab community's communications. *International Journal, 67*(4), 915–929.

Fraser Institute, Centre for Aboriginal Policy Study. (2014). https://www.fraserinstitute.org/sites/default/files/myths-and-realities-of-first-nations-education.pdf

Ganguly, I. (1995). Exploring the differences: Feminist theory in a multicultural society. *Hecate, 21*(1), 37.

Gibbon, J. M. (1938). *Canadian mosaic: The Making of a Northern Nation.* Toronto, Ontario, Canada: McLelland & Stewart.

Goldberg, D. T. (1993). *Racist culture: Philosophy and the politics of meaning.* Oxford, UK: Blackwell.

Graves, F. (2015, March 12). The EKOS poll: Are Canadians getting more racist? *iPolitics.* Retrieved December 5, 2015, from https://ipolitics.ca/2015/03/12/the-ekos-poll-are-canadians-getting-more-racist

Hall, J. R. (1992). The Capital(s) of Cultures: A Nonholistic Approach to Status, Situations, Class, Gender and Ethnicity. In Michel Lamont and Marcel Fournier (Eds.), *Cultivating Difference: Symbolic Boundaries and the Making of Inequality.* Chicago, IL: University of Chicago Press.

Hamadi, L. (2014). Edward Said: The postcolonial theory and the literature of decolonization. *Lebanon European Scientific Journal, 2,* 39–46.

Hanniman, W. (2008). Canadian Muslims, Islamophobia and national security. *International Journal of Law, Crime and Justice, 36*(4), 271–285.

Hedican, E. J. (2013). *Ipperwash: The tragic failure of Canada's Aboriginal policy.* Toronto, Ontario, Canada: University of Toronto Press.

Helly, D. (2004). Are Muslims discriminated against in Canada since September 2001? *Canadian Ethnic Studies, 36*(1), 24–47.

Henry, F., & Tator, C. (2006). *The colour of democracy: Racism in Canadian society.* 3rd Ed. Toronto: Nelson.

Henry, F., & Tator, C. (2009). *Racism in the Canadian university demanding social justice, inclusion, and equity.* Toronto, Ontario, Canada: University of Toronto Press.

Hoedl, K. (1997). Physical characteristics of the Jew. *Jewish Studies.* Retrieved October 6, 2015, from http://web.ceu.hu/jewishstudies/pdf/01_hoedl.pdf

Hogarth, K. (2011). Contested belonging: The experiences of racialized immigrant women in Canada. *International Journal of Diversity in Organizations, Communities and Nations, 10*(5), 63–74.

Hogarth, K. (2015). Home without security and security without home. *Journal of International Migration and Integration, 16,* 783–798. doi:10.1007/s12134-014-0367-z

hooks, b. (2000). *Feminist theory: From margin to center.* Boston, MA: South End Press.

Hurtado, A. (1999). *The color of privilege: Three blasphemies on race and feminism.* Ann Arbor, MI: University of Michigan Press.

Jakubowski, L. M. (1997). *Immigration and the legalization of racism.* Halifax, Nova Scotia, Canada: Fernwood.

Johnson, J. P., Lenartowicz, T., & Apud, S. (2006). Cross-cultural competence in international business: Toward a definition and a model. *Journal of International Business Studies, 37,* 525–543. doi:10.1057/palgrave.jibs.8400205

Kant, I. (1961). *Observations on the feeling of the beautiful and sublime* (J. T. Goldthwait, Trans.). University of California Press. (Original work published 1764)

Karam, E. (1935, August). Syrian immigration to Canada. *Syrian Canadian National Review, 19*–37.

Kashmeri, Z. (1991). *The gulf within: Canadian Arabs, racism, and the Gulf War.* Toronto, Ontario, Canada: Lorimer.

Kinsman, G., Steedman, M., & Buse, D. K. (2000). *Whose national security? Canadian state surveillance and the creation of enemies.* Toronto, Ontario, Canada: Between the Lines.

Kivisto, P. (2003). Social spaces, transnational immigrant communities and the politics of incorporation. *Ethnicities, 3*(1), 5–28.

Kripalani, S., Bussey-Jones, J., Katz, M. G., & Genao, I. (2006). A prescription for cultural competence in medical education. *Journal of General Internal Medicine, 21*(10), 1116–1120. doi:10.1111/j.1525-1497.2006.00557.x

Kutty, F. (2001). Muslims and Arabs in Canada feel racist backlash after terrorist attacks. *Washington Report on Middle East Affairs, XX*(8), 53.

Lee, E. O. J., & Brotman, S. (2011). Identity, Refugeeness, Belonging: Experiences of Sexual Minority Refugees in Canada. *Canadian Review of Sociology, 48*(3), 241–274.

Legare, E. (1995). Canadian multiculturalism and Aboriginal people: Negotiating a place in the nation. *Identities, 1*(4), 347–366.

Loomba, A. (2015). *Colonialism–postcolonialism* (3rd ed.). New York, NY: Routledge.

Lowell, B. L., Findlay, A., & Stewart, E. (2004). *Brain strain: Optimising highly skilled migration from developing countries* (Asylum and Migration Working Paper No. 3). London, UK: Institute for Public Policy Research.

Macdonald, D., & Wilson, D. (2013). *Poverty or prosperity: Indigenous children in Canada.* Retrieved October 12, 2015, from https://www.policyalternatives.ca/publications/reports/poverty-or-prosperity

Madibbo, A. I. (2006). *Minority within a minority: Black Francophone immigrants and the dynamics of power and resistance.* New York, NY: Routledge.

Mascarenhas, M. (2012). *Where the waters divide: Neoliberalism, White privilege, and environmental racism in Canada.* Lanham, MD: Lexington Books.

McKenzie, D., & Gibson, J. (2010). *The economic consequences of "brain drain" of the best and brightest: Microeconomic evidence from five countries.* Policy Research Working Papers. doi.org/10.1596/1813-9450-5394

Milloy, J. S. (1998). *A national crime: The Canadian government and the residential school system 1879–1986.* Winnipeg, Manitoba, Canada: University of Manitoba Press.

Mills, S. (1998). Postcolonial feminist theory. In S. Jackson & J. Jones (Eds.), *Contemporary feminist theories* (pp. 98–112). Edinburgh, UK: Edinburgh University Press.

Mohanty, C. T. (1991). Under Western eyes: Feminist scholarship and colonial discourses. In C. T. Mohanty, A. Russo, & L. Torres (Eds.), *Third World women and the politics of feminism* (pp. 51–80). Bloomington, IN: Indiana University Press.

Mohanty, C. T. (2003). *Feminism without borders: decolonizing theory, practicing solidarity.* London: Duke University Press.

Mosby, I. (2013, May). Administering colonial science: Nutrition and human biomedical experimentation in Aboriginal communities and residential school, 1942–1952. *Social History, 46*(91), 145–172.

Mosher, C. J. (1998). *Discrimination and denial: Systematic racism in Ontario's legal and criminal justice systems, 1892–1961.* Toronto, Ontario, Canada: University of Toronto Press.

Mosse, G. L. (1978). *Toward the final solution: A history of European racism.* New York, NY: Fertig.

Multicultural Health Broker Co-operative (2004). *All together now: A multicultural coalitional for equity in health and well-being: Final report.* Edmonton.

Narayan, U. (1997). *Dislocating cultures: Identities, traditions, and Third-World feminism.* New York, NY: Routledge.

Narayan, U. (2000). Essence of culture and a sense of history: A feminist critique of cultural essentialism. In: U. Narayan & S. Harding (Eds.), *Decentering the center* (pp. 80–100). Bloomington: Indiana UP.

Neibhur, R. H. (2004). *The social sources of denominationalism.* Whitefish, MT: Kessinger. (Original work published 1929)

Nelson, C. (2010). *Ebony roots, northern soil: Perspectives on Blackness in Canada.* Newcastle upon Tyne, UK: Cambridge Scholars.

Ogunade, A. O. (2011). *Human capital investment in the developing world: An analysis of praxis* (Seminar Series). Kingston, RI: Schmidt Labor Research Center, University of Rhode Island.

Ontario Human Rights Commission. (2005). Policy and guidelines on racism and racial discrimination. Retrieved from http://www.ohrc.on.ca/sites/default/files/attachments/Policy_and_guidelines_on_racism_and_racial_discrimination.pdf

Pecic, Z. (2013). *Queer narratives of the Caribbean diaspora: exploring tactics.* Houndmills, Basingstoke, Hampshire: Palgrave Macmillan.

Pollack, S. (2004). Anti-oppressive social work practice with women in prison: Discursive reconstructions and alternative practices. *British Journal of Social Work, 34,* 693–707.

Porter, J. (Ed.). (2015). *Vertical mosaic: Analysis of social class and power: 50th anniversary edition.* Toronto, Ontario, Canada: University of Toronto Press.

Portes, A. (1999). The study of transnationalism: Pitfalls and promise of an emergent research field. *Ethnic and Racial Studies, 22*(2), 217–237.

Potocky, M. (1997). Multicultural social work in the United States. *International Social Work, 40,* 315–326.

Prentice, A. (1977). *The school promoters.* Toronto, Ontario, Canada: McClelland & Stewart.

Ramirez, R. (2007). Race, tribal nation, and gender: A native feminist approach to belonging. *Meridians: Feminism, Race, Transnationalism, 7*(2), 22–40.

Razack, N., & Jeffery, D. (2002). Critical race discourse and tenets for social work. *Canadian Social Work Review, 19*(2), 257–271.

Redhead, M. (2002). *Charles Taylor: Thinking and living deep diversity.* Boston, MA: Rowman & Littlefield.

Richardson, B., Richardson, R., & Richardson, B. (2000). One family, indivisible? In C. E. James (Ed.), *Experiencing difference* (pp. 114–123). Halifax, Nova Scotia, Canada: Fernwood.

Rousseau, J. J. (1754). *A discourse on inequality.* London, UK: Penguin.

Said, E. (1978). *Orientalism.* London, UK: Penguin.

Said, E. (1984). Reflections on Exile and Other Essays.

Schiele, J. H. (2007). Implications of the equality-of-oppressions paradigm for curriculum content on people of color. *Journal of Social Work Education, 43,* 83–100.

Shamai, S. (1997). Jewish resistance to Christianity in the Ontario Public School System. *Historical Studies in Education, 9*(2), 251–255.

Shelley-Robinson, C. (2004). *Finding a place in the sun: The immigrant experience in Caribbean youth literature.* Jamaica: University of the West Indies.

Simms, G. P. (1993). Racism as a barrier. In W. Kaplan (Ed.), *Belonging: The meaning and future of Canadian citizenship* (pp. 333–348). Montreal, Quebec, Canada: McGill-Queen's University Press.

Sinclair, R. (2007). Identity lost and found: Lessons from the sixties scoop. *First Peoples Child & Family Review, 3*(1), 65–82.

Smith, B. (1991). The truth that never hurts: Black lesbians in fiction in the 1980s. In C. T. Mohanty, A. Russo, & L. Torres (Eds.), *Third World women and the politics of feminism* (pp. 101–132). Bloomington, IN: Indiana University Press.

Smith, M. P., & Guarnizo, L. (Eds.). (2002). *Transnationalism from below.* New Brunswick, NJ: Transaction Publishers.

Smith, R. C. (2002). Transnational localities: Community, technology and the politics of membership within the context of Mexico and U.S. migration. In M. P. Smith & L. Guarnizo (Eds.), *Transnationalism from below* (pp. 196–238). New Brunswick, NJ: Transaction Publishers.

Smith, T. (2014). (Re)turning home: An exploration in the (re)claiming of identity and belonging. In G. Sefa Dei & M. McDermott (Eds.), *Politics of anti-racism education: In search of strategies for transformative learning* (pp. 191–210). New York, NY: Springer.

Spivak, G. C. (1999). *A critique of postcolonial reason: Toward a history of the vanishing present.* Cambridge, MA: Harvard University Press.

Stark, O. (2002). *The economics of the brain drain turned on its head.* Paper presented at the ABCDE Europe Conference, Oslo, Norway.

Statistics Canada. (2013a). *Immigration and ethnocultural diversity in Canada: National household survey, 2011.* Retrieved January 15, 2016, from http://www12.statcan.gc.ca/nhs-enm/2011/as-sa/99-010-x/99-010-x2011001-eng.pdf

Statistics Canada. (2013b). *2011 national household survey: Aboriginal peoples in Canada: First Nations People, Métis and Inuit.* Retrieved from http://www.statcan.gc.ca/daily-quotidien/130508/dq130508a-eng.htm?HPA

Statistics Canada. (2015). Analysis of the Canadian immigrant labour market, 2008 to 2011. Retrieved January 20, 2017 http://www.statcan.gc.ca/pub/71-606-x/2012006/part-partie1-eng.htm

Stoffman, D. (2002). *Who gets in: What's wrong with Canada's immigration program—and how to fix it.* Toronto, Ontario, Canada: Macfarlane Walter & Ross.

Stuurman, S. (2000). Francois Bernier and the invention of racial classification. *History Workshop Journal, 2000*(50), 1–21.

Sun, K. (2015, August). *Foreign investment in real estate in Canada* [Occasional Papers Series Vol. 2, Issue 3]. Edmonton, Alberta, Canada: China Institute, University of Alberta.

Teferra, D. (2004). Brain Circulation: Unparalleled opportunities, underlying challenges and outmoded presumptions. *Journal of Studies in International Education, 9*(3), 229–250.

Thompson, C. (2015). Cultivating narratives of race, faith, and community: The dawn of tomorrow, 1923–1971. *Canadian Journal of History, 50*(1), 30–67.

Thornhill, E. M. A. (2008). So seldom for us, so often against us. *Journal of Black Studies, 38*(3), 321–337.

Tisdall, F. F., & Kruse, H. D. (1942, March 15). *Summary of findings from a nutritional survey of 300 Indians.* Library and Archives Canada, RG 29, Vol. 936, File 386-6-10.

Trudel, M. (1994). *Dictionnaire des esclaves et de leurs propriétaires au Canada français* (2nd ed. revised & amended). Montréal, Quebec, Canada: Hurtubise.

Truth and Reconciliation Commission. (2015). *Final report of the Truth and Reconciliation Commission, Volume 1: Summary.* Toronto, Ontario, Canada: Lorimer.

Verjee, Z. (2015). The Performing Identities of Muslims. In N. Aziz (Ed.), *The Relevance of Islamic Identity in Canada: Culture, Politics and Self.* Ontario: Mawenzi House Publishers.

Waligórska, M. (2013). *Music, longing and belonging: articulations of the self and the other in the musical realm.* Newcastle upon Tyne: Cambridge Scholars Pub.

Walker, J. W. S. G. (1985). *Racial discrimination in Canada: The Black experience.* Ottawa, Ontario, Canada: Canadian Historical Association.

Walkom, T. (2003, August 29). Suspicions win the day in absence of evidence. *Toronto Star.*

Wallis, M. A., Galabuzi, G.-E., & Sunseri, L. (2010). *Colonialism and racism in Canada: Historical traces and contemporary issues.* Toronto, Ontario, Canada: Nelson Education.

Wane, N. N. (2006). Is decolonization possible? In G. J. S. Dei & A. Kempf (Eds.), *Anti-colonialism and education: A politics of resistance* (pp. 87–106). Rotterdam, the Netherlands: Sense Publishers.

Weinfeld, M. (2002). *Like everyone else . . . but different: The paradoxical success of Canadian Jews.* Toronto, Ontario, Canada: McClelland & Stewart.

Winks, R. W. (1971). *Blacks in Canada: A history.* New Haven, CT: Yale University Press.

Wolfe, P. (2006). Settler colonialism and the elimination of the native. *Journal of Genocide Research, 8*(4), 387–409. doi:10.1080/14623520601056240

Woodsworth, J. S. (1909). *Strangers within our gates: Or coming Canadians.* Toronto, Ontario, Canada: Stephenson.

Yee, J. Y. (2005). Critical anti-racism praxis: The concept of Whiteness implicated. In S. Hick, J. Fook, & R. Pozzuto (Eds.), *Social work: A critical turn* (pp. 87–103). Toronto, Ontario, Canada: Thompson.

Index

Figures and boxes are indicated by an italic *f* and *b* following the page number.

Abella, I., 76
abolishment of slavery, 73, 102
Aboriginal people. *See* Indigenous people
Abu-Lughod, L., 110
academia, colonialism in, 42–44
Act to Grant Equal Rights and Privileges to Persons of the Jewish Religion, 78, 105
Act to Limit Slavery in Upper Canada, 73
Act to Restrict and Regulate Chinese Immigration into Canada, 58
adaptation
    of Arab and Muslim communities, 108–109
    of Black communities, 101–104
    of Chinese communities, 106–107
    of immigrant groups, 93–97
    of Japanese communities, 107–108
    of Jewish communities, 104–106
Africville, displacement of population of, 74
Ahmed, S., 64, 65, 88
Aladdin, 108–109
Alberta, rise of Social Credit Party in, 79
Alfred, G. T., 116n32
al-Qaeda sleeper cells, 84

Alvarez, L., 66
American War of Independence, 6
Anand, S. S., 15
Anthias, F., 91
anti-immigrant racism, 11–12
anti-racism, 19–21, 69, 109
antisemitism
    Canadian, 79–81
    Christie Pits riot, 79–80
    in history, 74–76
    racialized, 76–78
    recent surge in, 81
Anti-Slavery Society of Canada, 102
Anti-terrorism Act, 83
apartheid system, South Africa, 29
apology for residential schools, 39, 99–100*b*
Appadurai, A., 68
Arab immigrants
    adaptation of, 108–109
    multiculturalism and, 81–82
    racism towards, 13–16
    Syrian refugees, 13–14, 82, 84
assimilation. *See also* residential schools
    apology for, 99–100*b*
    education as tool for, 30–37
    government commitment to, 27–28

assimilation (*cont.*)
   of immigrants, 40, 56–57
   in immigration policies, 96
   of Jews, 77

Backhouse, C., 59
BADC (Black Action Defence Committee), 104
Bannerji, H., 54
ban on Indian ceremonies, 29, 32
Bauman, Z., 55
Beiser, M., 87
belonging
   adaptation and, 93–97
   Arab and Muslim communities, 108–109
   Black community, adaptation of, 101–104
   challenges of diaspora, 64–66
   changing notions of diaspora, 66–67
   Chinese community, adaptation of, 106–107
   citizenship and, 54–55
   difference, multiculturalism, and, 85–93
   effects of migration on, 64
   First Nation adaptation, 97–101
   Japanese community, adaptation of, 107–108
   negotiating, 50–51*b*
   racialized immigrants, 12–13
   social impacts of racism, 21
   spaces of, 111–112, 112*f*
Bernier, F., 4
Bhabha, H., 93
Bibb, H., 102
Bill 60, 40
Bill C-31, 32–33
Bill C-45, 101, 118n1
Bill C-51, 83
Bissonnette, A., 14
Bissoondath, N., 89
Black Action Defence Committee (BADC), 104

Black dangerousness, 11, 64
Blacks
   adaptation of community, 101–104
   Africville, displacement of population of, 74
   criminalization of, 11
   diaspora, 63–64
   employment rates, 90
   institutional racism against, 10–11
   multiculturalism, 72–74
   negotiating belonging, 50–51*b*
   racism in Canadian history, 9–11
   resistance efforts of, 102–104, 103*b*
   segregation of, 10, 63, 73–74
   slavery, 9–10, 38, 63, 72–73
   Viola Desmond case, 102, 103*b*
Blackstock, C., 115n15
Blair, F. C., 76, 77
blood purity, 75
BNA. *See* British North America
B'Nai Brith Society of Canada, 81
Bodvarsson, O., 8
brain drain, 41, 115n24
Bridge Initiative, 84
British Columbia
   Chinese immigration due to Gold Rush, 57–58
   movement of Japanese Canadians during WWII, 61–62
British Royal Proclamation of 1763, 26
British North America (BNA)
   abolishment of slavery, 73
   colonization, 6–7, 26–28
Bryce, Peter, 31
Bureau of Indian Affairs, United States, 30
Burton, P., 81
Bussey-Jones, J., 116n28

Calliste, A., 12
Canadian Air Transport Security Authority Act, 83
Canadian Constitution, 16–17
Canadian context, racism in, 6–9

Canadian Council of Churches, 62
Canadian identity, 57, 70
Canadian Jewish Congress, 78, 79
Canadian Mosaic: The Making of a Northern Nation (Gibbon), 70
Canadian Nationalist Party, 80
Canadian Pacific Railroad, 41, 57–58
Canadian Security Intelligence Service (CSIS), 83
Cardan, P., 7
carding, 104, 118n2
Caribbean peoples, 64
Castoriadis, C., 7
categorizations, 54
Catholics, participation in Christie Pits riot, 79–80
Caucasian Euro-descent normativity, 4, 6, 57
Certificates of Possession (CPs), 29
Charter of Rights and Freedoms, Canadian, 16–17
child welfare system, 39, 115n15, 115n16
Chinatowns, 107
Chinese immigrants
  adaptation of communities, 106–107
  Chinatowns, 107
  diaspora, 57–60
  entrepreneurship, 106
  head tax on, 58, 60
  threat to Canadian identity, 57
  work on Canadian Pacific Railroad, 41, 57–58
Chinese Immigration Act, 60
Christianity, 75, xi–xii
Christie Pits riot, 79–80
citizenship, 54–55, 71
civilizing mission, 14
Clearing the Plains: Disease, Politics of Starvation, and the Loss of Aboriginal Life (Daschuk), 37–38
climate requirement in immigration act, 8
colonial education, 42

colonialism, 23–24
  in academia, 42–44
  in Canadian policies, 37–42
  colonization in Canadian context, 24–26
  concept of racial classification in, 4–5
  criminalization of Indigenous culture, 29
  education as assimilationist tool, 30–37
  impact on First Nations, 26–28, 116n32
  Indian Act, 28–29
  multiculturalism as tool for, 88
  reserve lands, 29–30
  in Western feminist discourse, 44–47
colonization of Canada, 6–8, 24–26
Common School Act of 1850, 10
Community: Seeking Safety in an Insecure World (Bauman), 55
Confederation, 27
Constitution, Canadian, 16–17
counternarratives, 98
CPs (Certificates of Possession), 29
criminalization
  of Blacks, 11, 64
  of Indigenous culture, 29, 32
  normalizing of Whiteness, 20
criminal justice system, racism in, 15–17
critical multiculturalism, 92
CSIS (Canadian Security Intelligence Service), 83
cultural competency, 43–44, 116n28
Cuvier, G., 4

Daschuk, J., 37–38
Davin Commission, 30–31
de Beauvior, S., 2
Dei, G. S., 19
Department of Indian Affairs (DIA), 25, 28
Depression, 31, 79
deracializing of policies, 10, 63
Desmond, V., 102, 103*b*
developing countries, immigration from, 41–42

DIA (Department of Indian Affairs), 25, 28
diaspora, 49–52
  assimilation of immigrants, 56–57
  Black experience, 63–64
  challenges of, 64–66
  Chinese immigrants, 57–60
  connection to home countries, 65–66
  e-diaspora, 67–68
  Japanese immigrants, 60–63
  laws defining space by race, 55–56
  negotiating belonging, 50–51*b*
  shifting notions of, 66–68
  space and social imaginary, 52–55
  understanding, 52
diasporic public sphere, 68
difference
  belonging, multiculturalism and, 85–93
  mosaic image of Canadian identity, 70
Diminescu, D., 67
Discourse on Inequality, A (Rousseau), 4
discrimination. *See also* racism
  of Blacks, 11, 64, 72
  immigration policy, 8
  of Jews, 75
  in multiculturalism, 92
  religious justification of, 75
  systemic racism, 109
  towards Muslims, 13
diversity
  cultural competency, 43–44, 116n28
  multiculturalism and, 71, 88, 92
  Quebec Charter of Values, 14
Dunbar, W., 3

e-diaspora, 67–68
education. *See also* residential schools
  as assimilationist tool, 27, 30–37
  of Blacks, 101
  colonial, 42–44
  of First Nation children, 98
  of Japanese Canadians, 107
  social lift, 97
embedded social hierarchy, x
Enlightenment, 2–3
entrepreneurship of Chinese immigrants, 106
equality rights, 16
ethnocentric universalism, 45–46
eugenics, 76
Euro-decent Caucasian classification, 4, 6, 57
Exclusion Act, 60

face coverings, ban on, 40
family food allowances for Indigenous peoples, 25
family reunification of Chinese immigrants, 60
famine, politics of, 38
Feagin, J., 109
feminist discourse, colonial reproduction in, 44–47
Fine, M., 88–89
First Nations
  adaptation of, 97–101
  colonialism, 26–28
  criminalization of Indigenous culture, 29
  education as assimilationist tool, 30–37
  government apology for residential schools, 99–100*b*
  Idle No More, 101
  impact of colonialism, 116n32
  Indian Act, 28–29
  policy of friendship, 26–27
  reserve lands, 29–30
  voting rights for, 32
First World scholarship, 43
Fletcher, Wendy L., xix–xxi
food allowances for Indigenous peoples, 25
Foucault, M., 52–53, 97

friendship, policy of, 26–27
"From Sea to Sea" motto, ix
Fugitive Slave Act of 1850, 73

Ganguly, I., 45
Genao, I., 116n28
gender
    challenges of diaspora, 66
    feminist discourse, 44–47
    Muslim resistance, 109
    workplace legislation for White women, 59
Gibbon, J. M., 70
global deterritorialization, 69
globalization, 49, 67–68
Gold Rush in British Columbia, 57–58
Gradual Civilization Act of 1857, 27, 28

halfies, 110
Hanniman, W., 13
Hardie, S., 114n11
Harper, S., 39, 60, 99–100b
Hart, E., 105
head tax on Chinese immigrants, 58, 60
health of First Nations people, 37–38
Hedican, E. J., 111
hegemony
    defined, xi
    education, 97
    multiculturalism, 72
    through policies of multiculturalism, 89–90
heterotopia, 52–54
hijab, 109
Hill, W., 34b
Hindu problem, 57
historical narratives, xi
Hitler, A., 76
Hogarth, K., xvii–xix
    "On Fighting the Beast", xxi
    "Prisoner Scream", 21–22
    "Token Ism", 48

Holocaust, 75–77
home countries, connection of diasporic groups to, 65–66
homogeneity, 55, x

ICTs (information and communication technologies), 67–68
ideal of multiculturalism, 91–92
Idle No More, 101, 118n1
immigration. *See also* diaspora; *specific immigrant groups*
    after American independence, 6–7
    assimilation of immigrants, 40, 56–57, 96
    brain drain, 41–42
    from Britain, 7–8
    categorization of, 54
    e-diaspora, 67–68
    history of racism in, 2–6
    immigration act of 1910, 8
    microcultures, 96
    multiculturalism, problems caused by, 89–90
    opposition to, 113n4
    policy changes after WWII, 8–9
    racism in modern, 11–13
    reproduction of colonialism in policy, 40–42
    sense of belonging, 64
    social lift, 97
    space by race, 55–56
    unemployment of immigrants, 90
Immigration Act, 40–41
imperialism, concept of racial classification in, 4–5
inclusion, 22, 66, 87, 110
Indian Act
    Bill C-31, 32–33
    criminalization of Indigenous culture, 29, 32
    limitations under, 28–29
    reserve lands, 29–30

Indian problem, 30, 39
Indigenous people. *See also* Indian Act;
    residential schools
  adaptation of, 97–101
  child welfare policies affecting, 39
  criminalization of culture, 29, 32
  current challenges facing, 33
  death of Brian Sinclair, 95*b*
  effect of migration after American
    independence on, 6–7
  family food allowances, 25
  idealized idea of, 3–4
  idea of during colonial expansion, 5
  Idle No More, 101
  multiculturalism and, 90
  "one drop rule", 38
  potlatch ceremonies, 29
  poverty of, 40
  reserve lands, 29–30
  systemic neglect of, 95*b*
  voting rights for, 32
information and communication
    technologies (ICTs), 67–68
institutional racism, 10–11
integration
  multiculturalism policy, 87, 89, 91
  of racialized immigrants, 12
Internet, diaspora through. *See*
    e-diaspora
internment of Japanese Canadians during
    WWII, 61–62, 107–108
interrogation of Whiteness, 20
intersectionality of oppressions, 20
invisibility of racism, 20
Irish potato famines, 7
Islam. *See* Muslims
Islamophobia, 13, 82–85

Japanese immigrants
  adaptation of communities, 107–108
  diaspora, 60–63
  threat to Canadian identity, 57
Jews
  adaption and resilience of
    communities, 104–106
  antisemitism, 74–76
  Canadian antisemitism, 79–81
  Canadian refusal of Jewish refugees
    during Holocaust, 76–77
  Christie Pits riot, 79–80
  discrimination against, 80–81
  immigration into Canada, 78–79
  racialized antisemitism, 76–78
  use of race as category, 3
Jobs and Growth Act, 118n1

Kant, I., 4
Katz, M. G., 116n28
King, W. L. M., 8–9, 61, 77
Kripalani, S., 116n28
Kruse, H. D., 25
Ku Klux Klan, 103–104

Lacroix, W., 77
Laurier, W., 56
Legare, E., 86–87
legislation
  abolishing slavery, 73
  anti-terrorism, 83
  Chinese Immigration Act, 60
  defining space by race, 55–56
  history of racism, 15–17
  limiting Chinese immigration, 58
  against racism, negative effect of, 21
  regarding Jewish immigrants, 78
  White Woman's Labour Law, 59
  Zero Tolerance for Barbaric Cultural
    Practices Act, 84
Like Everyone Else But Different
    (Weinfeld), 87
Lloyd, C., 91
Loomba, A., 37

Macdonald, D., 40
MacDonald, J. A., 28
Maclean's magazine, 81
media, role in anti-Muslim racism, 13
men. *See* gender
MI (Mohawk Institute), 34–36, 34*b*, 36*b*, 114n11
microcultures, 96
Millennium Scoop, 39
Mills, S., 47
Mohanty, C. T., 45–46, 47
Mohawk Institute (MI), 34–36, 34*b*, 36*b*, 114n11
mosaic image of Canadian identity, 70
Mosby, I., 24
Mulroney, B., 61–62
Multicultural Health Broker Co-operative, 89
multiculturalism, 70–72
   Arabs, 81–82
   Black Canadians, 72–74
   critical, 92
   criticism of policy, 85–93
   difference, belonging, and, 85–93
   Islamophobia, 82–85
   Jews
      antisemitism, 74–76
      Canadian antisemitism, 79–81
      immigration into Canada, 78–79
      racialized antisemitism, 76–78
   maintenance of heritage and cultures, 85–86
   national unity and, 86–87
   official policy of, 70–72, 85–88
   problems for immigrants, 89–90
   terminologies embedded within, 91
music-related diaspora, 66–67
Muslims
   adaptation of communities, 108–109
   exclusion from diaspora, 66
   face coverings, ban on, 40
   increase in immigration of, 113n5
   Islamophobia, 82–85
   racism, 13–16
   use of hijab, 109

Narayan, U., 46–47
National Fascism Convention (1938), 80
National Socialism in Germany, 75–77
Native Sons of Canada, 79
Neibhur, H. R., 97
new racism, 116n27
niqab, 40
"No Jews Need Apply" (Burton), 81
None Is Too Many (Abella, Toper), 76
non-racist space, 92–93, 109
normativeness
   assimilation of immigrants, 56–57
   Caucasian Euro-descent, 4, 6, 57
   Christianity, 75
   of Whiteness, 20, 88–89
nutritional experiments in Indigenous populations, 24–25

Observations on the Feeling of the Beautiful and the Sublime (Kant), 4
Ogunade, A. O., 115n21
"one drop rule", 38
"On Fighting the Beast" (Hogarth), xxi
oppression
   anti-racism, 19
   cultural competency, 44
   intersectionality of, 20
   multiculturalism and, 90
   race as tool of, 2–3
   social lift, 97
Other
   anti-immigrant racism, 11–12
   antisemitism, 74–75
   colonial education, 42–44

Other (cont.)
　effect of racism and anti-racism, 21
　feminist discourse, 45–47
　misrecognition of, 111
　multiculturalism, 86
　negotiating belonging, 50–51b
　racialization, 2
　use of terms to characterize, 54

persistence of Japanese Canadians, 107–108
personal racism, 109
Pietism, 2–3
point-based selection system, 41, 115n22, 115n23
politics of famine, 38
post-colonial feminists, 47
potlatch ceremonies, 29
poverty in Indigenous communities, 40, 115n20
Presse, La, 77
"Prisoner Scream" (Hogarth), 21–22
prison population, percentage of Blacks in, 11
"Project Thread", 84

quality of life, racism and, 17–18b
Quebec, Jewish communities in, 104–105
Quebec Charter of Values, 14, 40

RACAR (Riverdale Action Committee Against Racism), 104
race
　in census categories, 55
　defining, 1
　roots of idea, 2–5
　saliency of, 20
racial classification, 4–5
racialization, defining, 1–2
racialized
　antisemitism, 75, 76–78
　defining, 1–2
　effect of racism and anti-racism, 21
　immigrant migration, 12
　internalization of identities, 64–65
racial profiling, 11, 13
racism, 1–2. *See also* antisemitism
　anti-Black, 63
　anti-Japanese, 61–62
　anti-racism, 19–21
　Black history in Canada, 9–11
　Canadian context, 6–9
　defining, 1, 5
　in everyday life, 17–18b
　in history of diaspora in Canada, 69
　immigration and refugees, 11–13
　invisibility of, 20
　Islamophobia, 82–83
　Ku Klux Klan, 103–104
　legal changes regarding, 16–17
　Muslim and Arab Canadians, 13–16
　negotiating belonging, 50–51b
　new, 116n27
　personal, 109
　systemic, 109
　in Western culture and Canadian immigration, 2–6
Racist America: Roots, Current Realities, and Future (Feagin), 109
Redhead, M., 87
refugees
　racism towards, 11–13
　refusal of Jewish immigrants during Holocaust, 76–77
　Syrian, 13–14, 82, 84
religion, xi–xii. *See also* Jews; Muslims
　anti-Japanese racism, 62
　assimilation of immigrants, 56–57
　in Black communities, 101–102
　blood purity concept, 75
　Christianity, 75, xi–xii
　Islam, media portrayal of, 13
　religious symbols, banning of, 14

roots of concept of race, 2–3
separation between church and state, 105
relocation of Japanese Canadians during WWII, 61–62, 107–108
representation, in feminist discourse, 45
reserve lands, 29–30
residential schools
  apology for, 39, 99–100*b*
  closure of, 32
  colonialism and, 38–39
  conditions in, 31, 34–35
  creation of, 30–31
  education at, 35
  legacy of, 98
  Mohawk Institute, 34–36, 34*b*, 36*b*, 114n11
  nutritional experiments in, 24–25
  Truth and Reconciliation Commission, 98
  underfunding of, 31, 35
resilience, 93–94
  of Arab and Muslim communities, 108–109
  of Chinese communities, 106–107
  of Japanese communities, 107–108
  of Jewish communities, 104–106
resistance movements, 20, 102–104, 103*b*
Richardson, B., 15
Richardson, R., 15
Riverdale Action Committee Against Racism (RACAR), 104
romanticism, 3–4
Rousseau, J. J., 4

Said, E., 42
saliency of race, 20
scholarship, flow of, 43
schools, residential. *See* residential schools
school system, segregation of Chinese immigrants in, 60
SCP (Social Credit Party), 79

security state, 14
segregation, 9, 10
  of Blacks, 63, 73–74
  of Chinese immigrants, 60
  impact of, 113n3
  Viola Desmond case, 102, 103*b*
selection system for immigrants, 41, 115n22, 115n23
self-government, Aboriginal, 26, 28, 98
Selling Illusions: The Cult of Multiculturalism (Bissoondath), 89
separation between church and state, 105, xi
September 11, 2001 (9/11), 13, 82–83
Seven Years' War, 6
sexual minorities as diaspora communities, 67
Shelley-Robinson, C., 64
Sinclair, B., 95*b*
Sinclair, R., 115n16
Six Nations Reserve, 7
Sixties Scoop, 39
skin color, racial classification based on, 4
slavery
  abolishment of, 73
  of Blacks in Canada, 9–10, 63, 72–73
  effect on Caribbean peoples, 64
  legal foundation, 113n1
  one drop rule, 38
  racial classification, 5
  resistance efforts, 102
Smith, B., 44–45
Smith, E., 36*b*
Social Credit Party (SCP), 79
social engagement, 105
social imaginary
  in Canada, 7, 8, 17
  changes after WWII, 9
  multiculturalism, 70, 72, 91–93
  space and, 52–55
social lift, 97

social networks, diaspora through, 67–68
Soja, E., 53
South African apartheid system, 29
space
  of belonging, 112*f*
  challenges of diaspora, 64–66
  heterotopia, 52–54
  laws defining, 55–56
  negotiating belonging, 50–51*b*
  non-racist, 92–93
  and social imaginary, 52–55
Statistics Canada, 39, 90, 113n5
stereotypes, 57, 111
St. Louis (ship), 77
Stoffman, D., 89
Strange Encounters (Ahmed), 65
stranger-ness, 65, 68
Strangers at the Gate: The Boat People's First Ten Years in Canada (Beiser), 87
Strangers Within Our Gates (Woodworth), 56–57
strategic essentialism, x
Syrian refugees, 13–14, 82, 84
systemic racism, 109

TB (tuberculosis), 24–25
Teferra, D., 67–68
terrorism, 13–14, 82–83, 84
Third Space theory, 53, 93, 109
Third World feminist approach, 45–47
Tisdall, F. F., 25
"Token Ism" (Hogarth), 48
tolerance, concept of, 90–91, 96
Toper, H., 76
Toronto
  al-Qaeda sleeper cell investigations, 84–85
  Black community in, 101
  Christie Pits riot, 79–80
  National Fascism Convention (1938), 80

transnationalism, 49, 68
TRC (Truth and Reconciliation Commission), 24, 98, 114n13, 115n14
treaties, 26–27
Trudeau, J., 13–14
Trudeau, P., 70–71, 86
Truth and Reconciliation Commission (TRC), 24, 98, 114n13, 115n14
tuberculosis (TB), 24–25

Underground Railroad, 10
unemployment of immigrants, 90
Universal Declaration of Human Rights, 9, 15, 32
universalism in feminist discourse, 45–47

Van den Berg, H., 8
Verjee, Z., 108
Voice of the Fugitive, 102
voting rights, 32, 55, 60

Waligórska, M., 66–67
Walker, J., 63–64
Walker, J. W. S. G., 10
Wane, N. N., 42–43
War on Terror, 108
Weinfeld, M., 87
Western culture
  colonial education, 42–44
  feminist discourse, 44–47
  history of racism in, 2–6
White fragility, 21
Whites
  colonial education, 42–44
  immigration discourse, 11–12
  interrogation of Whiteness, 20
  legalized segregation, 10
  negotiating belonging, 50–51*b*
  normativity of Whiteness, 19, 88–89
  superiority in racial classification, 4–5
  workplace legislation for women, 59

White Woman's Labour Law, 59
Who Gets In (Stoffman), 89
Wilson, D., 40
Winks, R. W., 113n1
women
    feminist discourse, colonial reproduction in, 44–47
    Muslim resistance, 109
    Viola Desmond case, 102, 103*b*
    workplace legislation for White women, 59
Woodworth, J. S., 56–57
workplace legislation for White women, 59

World Happiness Report, United Nations General Assembly, 115n19
World War II
    immigration policy after, 8–9
    racialized antisemitism, 75–77
    treatment of Japanese Canadians during, 61–62

xenophobia, 12

Zero Tolerance for Barbaric Cultural Practices Act, 84